REF
TD
159
.A1
F68
Cop. 1

Fox, Herbert

Urban technology

DATE DUE

URBAN TECHNOLOGY

A Second Primer on Problems

URBAN PROBLEMS AND URBAN TECHNOLOGY SERIES

SERIES EDITOR

Herbert Fox

Division of Science and Technology
New York Institute of Technology
Old Westbury, New York

Volume 1: Urban Technology: A Primer on Problems
Volume 2: Urban Technology: A Second Primer on Problems

Other Volumes in Preparation

URBAN TECHNOLOGY

A Second Primer on Problems

Herbert Fox
Division of Science and Technology
New York Institute of Technology
Old Westbury, New York

MARCEL DEKKER, INC.   New York and Basel

MARCEL DEKKER, INC.

270 Madison Avenue, New York, New York 10016

LIBRARY OF CONGRESS CATALOG CARD NUMBER: 75-1686

ISBN : 0-8247-6295-9

Current printing (last digit):
10 9 8 7 6 5 4 3 2 1

PRINTED IN THE UNITED STATES OF AMERICA

TO DOROTHY

CONTENTS

ACKNOWLEDGMENTS

It is my pleasure to thank many of the people who contributed to the output described here. I must first thank the National Science Foundation which, under Grant GT-33083 to the American Institute of Aeronautics and Astronautics, provided support to the chairmen and to me for the preparation of this document. Particular gratitude is extended to Dr. M. Frank Hersman, Director of the Office on Intergovernmental Science Programs and to Robert Crawford and his staff.

I also thank Dr. Alexander Schure and Dr. Theodore K. Steele of the New York Institute of Technology for giving me the opportunity and encouragement to pursue this activity.

The coordination and efforts of the American Institute of Aeronautics and Astronautics, as provided by Dr. Jerry Grey and Miss Christine Krop, are sincerely appreciated.

The chairmen and their panels, as a group, worked diligently to produce much of the written material. I thank them for their considerable efforts.

I also express my gratitude to Mrs. Shirley Solow who carefully reviewed, edited and typed this manuscript.

Finally, I must add, however, that the conclusions and interpretations of the sessions are my own and I take full responsibility for them.

Herbert Fox
Old Westbury, N.Y.

With the excellent program developed for the Second Urban Technology Conference (UTC 2) in July 1972, the Third Urban Technology Conference (UTC 3) was undertaken in Boston in September, 1973. Like its predecessor, the goal of the conference was the continued growth in communications and understanding, between those who generate technology and those who use it.

The breadth of interest in this link in the system is again expressed by the extensive cosponsorship of the meeting. The meeting was organized and managed by the American Institute of Aeronautics and Astronautics and by Public Technology, Incorporated. The cosponsors included the American Institute of Chemical Engineers, the American Society of Civil Engineers, the American Society of Mechanical Engineers, the Institute of Electrical and Electronic Engineers, the National Association of Counties, the National Governors Conference, the National Society of Professional Engineers, the U.S. Conference of Mayors in conjunction with the International City Management Association, and the host city, Boston.

As in the past, this conference had three major segments: main plenary sessions organized to discuss five major themes through paper presentations and panel discussions; the working groups for detailed treatment of particular elements of the technology; and the display which featured exhibits of hardware, software, and programs from both the private and government sectors related to all aspects of an urban technology.

Our emphasis here will be on the presentations and subsequent discussions related to the working groups. For completeness, it may be worthwhile to review the other elements of the program so that the complete perspective of the conference may be seen. The five major themes of the plenary sessions run by a team of technologists and urban users were: balanced transportation for the city, effective design of municipal vehicles, the energy crisis of the 70's, protecting the environment, and urban management. Clearly, the prime problems facing the urban sector were addressed. A compendium of the papers presented is available from the American Institute of Aeronautics and Astronautics (1).

The technology display offered many of the ingredients essential to both the user and the developer. On the one hand, federal programs were described in detail so that local government representatives could learn what is available for them and private industry might better understand the directions and priorities being established for funding in research and development. On the other hand, the corporate displays provided the opportunity for these two sectors to discuss missions, specifications, and costs -- items pertinent to the marketplace and eventual technology transfer.

The concept of the working groups which was first tried at UTC 2 was extended and improved upon. (The summary of the results of the second conference is available in Reference 2.) The topical areas selected by a team from the American Institute of Aeronautics and Astronautics (AIAA), the National Science Foundation (NSF), and Public Technology, Inc. (PTI) were airport security, air and water pollution abatement utilizing Earth Observation Satellites, bus transportation, cable television franchising, education technology, fireground communications, medical care delivery systems, police vehicle performance specifications, power plant siting, and solid waste collection.

The mechanism used to generate both the working papers and the composition of the panels differed substantially from that employed for UTC 2. Here, the working group leadership, Herbert Fox and Jerry Grey of AIAA, Robert Crawford of NSF, and J. Robert Havlick and John Lawton of PTI, chose the themes and selected the chairman for each group. The bases for selection were prominence in his field and the ability to draw together a high level panel for the meeting. The chairman's job was to generate the working paper, select the panelists to discuss the topic, and then after the meeting, to create a summary of the session. A list of the working groups, their chairmen, and the panelists is displayed in the Appendix.

A rationale for the selection of some of the problems is perhaps in order. It will be noted that not all those treated in UTC 2 are repeated here. The session in firesafe building materials was deleted in favor of fireground communications. The latter appeared to be ripe for technological implementation and is high on the priority list of most cities. In place of liquid waste management (toxicity detection), a general session was substituted that discussed application of remote sensing for both air and water pollution abatements using the Earth Resource Technology Satellites (ERTS). The acquisition of police vehicles is treated here, combined with the market aggregation question of UTC 2; the law enforcement panel was eliminated so we could deal directly with vehicle technology.

Two other panels were deleted: computer sciences and management sciences. It was felt that these softer technologies were all-pervasive and impacted on almost every working group. Thus, we will see sophisticated management techniques being brought to bear in many areas discussed here; likewise, substantial computer applications for urban technologies have been developed and are cited within their particular context.

The problem areas reexamined at UTC 3 include emergency medical care delivery systems, solid waste management, cable television, and power plant siting. These four sessions treat topics of prime importance to local government, and it was felt that they deserved additional tracking at this third conference.

As pointed out at UTC 2, the technology for emergency health care exists but implementation is the problem; therefore, the panel session was devoted to inhibitors to the application of existing systems. Solid waste management still appears as the major problem for local government; new technologies and management techniques are exposed in that panel discussion. Many of the same problems suggested

at UTC 2 still arise in both cable television franchising and power
plant siting; further identification is needed to permit institutions
to develop new policy constructs to address these more effectively.
You will note that an essential element of these working groups is
continuity. Year-by-year discussions can show progress (or lack of
it) and suggest new directions and policies. More of this notion will
be discussed in Chapter 5.

The other new sessions introduced at this conference were educational technology, bus transportation systems, and airport security.
With increasing pressure at all levels on most school systems to be
more innovative and productive, it was felt that a session on educational technology would be more appropriate. In light of what probably will be a continuing energy problem for the United States, effective mass transit becomes ever more pertinent, and so the panel on
bus transportation was included. In this tutorial session, urban managers were exposed to a variety of techniques, suitable for immediate
implementation, to inexpensively improve their bus transportation systems. Because of the growing expenses borne by local airports as a
result of thefts and hijackings, it seemed important to include a session describing methods and government direction in maintaining airport security.

Basically, the charge to the panels was the same as at UTC 2.
Their job was to dissect the working document and decide if the problem, as stated, addressed the important issues. Discussion was to be
devoted to the problem and the inhibitors to the transfer of the technology. The panel and audience discussions were taped and annotated
by student reporters. These and the original problem statements form
the basis for this report.

To lend cohesiveness to these reviews the problem areas are separated, where possible, according to common threads as was done in the
first volume (Reference 2). The same elemental issue definitions are
used here to afford continuity and to emphasize that such a breakdown
is useful for discussion purposes.

The dominant issues which apply to the current crop of 10 working group discussions have therefore been placed in technology-intensive or policy-intensive categories. For technology-intensive problems, two subissues are highlighted: application of existing equipment* and development of new products*. The policy-intensive problems can also be divided into subissues: internal local government decisions needed for implementation, and actual political realities. The groups and their relation to this breakdown of issues are shown in Figure 1. In Chapters 1 and 2, the technology-intensive and policy-intensive issues, respectively, are treated in detail.

DOMINANT   ISSUES

TECHNOLOGY-INTENSIVE

APPLICATIONS	DEVELOPMENTS
AIRPORT SECURITY	EDUCATION
BUS TRANSPORT	ERTS
SOLID WASTE	FIRE COMMUNICATION
	POLICE VEHICLES

POLICY-INTENSIVE

INTERNAL	EXTERNAL
EMERGENCY MEDICAL CARE	CABLE TV
	POWERPLANT SITING

FIG. 1.   Dominant Issues

---

*In this context, the words "equipment" and "products" are used in their most general form and are taken to imply hardware or software where appropriate.

Some comment is pertinent here to pave the way for the interested reader. It should be observed that a uniform format for the panel discussions did not conveniently arise. However, this is not necessarily unfortunate. Many panels, offering relatively new material, operated more as tutorial sessions than as working groups. This is certainly valid since education and information transfer were prime motives for the sessions.

In addition, since there are 10 different authors and styles involved, it is impossible to present each problem area identically. (Recall that at UTC 2, a single author was responsible for generating all the written material.) The success of these new procedures for problem statements, summaries, and panel selection remains to be seen. Careful reading of the following chapters may indicate only spotty improvement. Further judgment and review will be left for the concluding chapters of this report.

Another item which will be dealt with in detail later is the actual choice of working group topics. This bears heavily on the ultimate utility of a particular panel. As at UTC 2, and as evident in Figure 1, emphasis was on the technological issues. Thus the panels discussed requirements and specifications. Clearly, more substantial discussion on the core problems in technology transfer and its inhibitors can arise from examination of the policy and nondevelopmental problems. Overall dissemination of available systems is surely hindered by emphasis on these technology-dominated working groups.

A problem area which has continually arisen throughout the several urban technology conferences is the nature of the disaggregated marketplace of local government. Partially in response to a need to better describe this arena and partially to amplify the subsequent discussion of inhibitors, a short chapter summarizing expenditures for typical urban problems is offered in Chapter 3.

Finally, in Chapter 4, a review of all the material is presented to emphasize and integrate several features; the first is a discussion of the inhibitors to the technology transfer, in relation to the marketplace, based on the working group materials, and the second is an overall evaluation of the working group concept as one mechanism among many to enhance the introduction of new technology to the urban sector.

REFERENCES

1. "A Collection of Technical Papers," Third Urban Technology Conference and Technical Display, Boston, Massachusetts, September 1973, American Institute of Aeronautics and Astronautics, New York.

2. Fox, H., "Urban Technology: A Primer on Problems," Vol. 1, Marcel Dekker, Inc., New York, 1973.

URBAN TECHNOLOGY

A Second Primer on Problems

Chapter 1

PROBLEMS: TECHNOLOGY-INTENSIVE

In this chapter we focus our attention on the actual workshops, their problem statements, and the summaries of the panel activities. These are presented according to the issue-oriented categories cited in the Introduction.

The first to be studied are those from which the urban sector can profit through application of the tools or technology. Airport security is a case in point. Hijacking and cargo thefts greatly affect local airport operations since costs associated with security must ultimately be paid by the local constituency. Application of modern techniques in response to Federal Aviation Administration directives appears effective and transferable regardless of locality.

Alternatives to the automobile in the form of innovative bus systems are examined next. A variety of programs aimed at increasing ridership by improving service at low-to-moderate cost permitting local government a choice of technologies was described. Detailed examples indicate the wealth of data available and demonstrate how these innovations can be used effectively.

We may note that in these sessions technology was viewed in its broadest form, including the soft, management science in its scope.

The working group on solid waste collection is included in the application section because much of the technology described is truly of this type -- computerized collection systems, new treatment plants, etc. It is also clear that considerable developmental work needs to be done in a variety of areas, notably in recycling and in collection equipment. Critical policy issues exist which must be overcome in

1

order to introduce to the existing technologies a degree of success. On balance, however, more extensive application is necessary.

Air and water pollution abatement using Earth Resource Technology Satellites epitomized the exotic transfer of technology from space to earth. The use of remote sensing from earth satellites may be the most cost-effective method for pollution detection and abatement. The purpose here was to expose the urban sector to this potential and to suggest the wealth of data and systems available. Here, developments are aimed at generation information useful for local governments in their operations.

The myriad tools of education technology have been touted as the wave of the future for improving the quality of classroom instruction while lowering cost. However, as pointed out, still better ones must be developed if these goals are to be met. The many policy issues which arise in the question of implementation were discussed because of their implications and possible impediment to the research and development process. More complete discussion must be deferred until these tools are, in fact, better developed.

Since traditional communication at the scene of a fire is greatly hampered, the importance of a light, highly portable means of effective fireground communication has been recognized for some time. This session was devoted to a discussion of problems, specifications, and needs. The panel and audience functioned as a user design committee in the best sense of a working group. In the future, this area will be tracked to see how closely developments approach the outline presented here.

Initially addressed at UTC 2, Police Vehicle Technology is emerging as a high priority matter. The purpose of the panel was to expose this issue to a new and larger audience and hopefully to make progress on several fronts -- to stress the importance of developing specifications to cover needs, to point out to industry that standard, off-the-shelf sedans are not the answer, and to note that local police forces need new and better equipment.

I. AIRPORT SECURITY

J. Donald Reilly

Airport Operators Council International
Washington, D.C.

PROBLEM STATEMENT

A safe, reliable, economically feasible and opera-
tionally acceptable system is needed to provide protection to persons and property in air transportation from hijacking, extortion and sabotage, and to
minimize cargo/property theft and pilferage.

A. BACKGROUND

1. Hijacking

Down through the ages the traveler has been faced with the possibility that the course of his journey could at any moment be altered
by hijackers, pirates, or robbers. No mode of transportation has been
immune -- from the days of the caravans in biblical times through the
days when pirates and buccaneers roamed the seas and waterways. Even
in the days of coach and early train travel, "shotgun guards" did not
guarantee a safe passage for the traveler and his possessions.

Traveling by aircraft had virtually eliminated the hold up hazard. But starting in 1948, hijacking was introduced as a means to
escape from the communist controlled countries of Europe. The hijackers were said to be heros and were granted political asylum. In
three years there were 13 such hijackings; then in the eight years
following 1950 there were only 2 hijackings, both political. In 1958
the situation in Korea and Cuba started a series of hijackings which,
eventually with the accompanying broad news coverage, was to show the
would-be hijacker the apparent way to greater riches and was to fos-
ter the growth of a new threat in the form of the extortionist, ter-
rorist, and saboteur. The resulting publicity also attracted the lu-

natic and publicity seeker. Although the majority of the hijackings were for political reasons, the simplicity of accomplishment, the degree of success, and lack of successful prosecution prompted an increase in the number of hijack attempts per year. In 1969 a total of 87 occurred throughout the world. Seventy of these were successful with 58 going to Cuba.

In only three of the years in which air hijackings have occurred since 1930 has the success rate been below 50%. Through 1960, 82% of the hijack attempts were successful.

Benjamin O. Davis, DOT Assistant Secretary for Safety and Consumer Affairs, explains the recent hijacking situation as follows:

> Phase One of the hijacking phenomenon was concerned with Cuba-bound refugees. Hijackings in this category constituted more of a nuisance than a real danger.
>
> Phase Two was the era of the extortionist -- calculated hijackings motivated by greed. The hijacker in this category was intrinsically more dangerous than his predecessor.
>
> In Phase Three, we encountered the fleeing felon -- a criminal not unwilling to add larceny or kidnapping or even murder perhaps, to his other illegal deeds. No type of hijacking is acceptable, but the desperate fugitive from justice undoubtedly poses the greatest threat to passenger and crew safety. His access to air transportation must be cut off.

The United States Congress in 1965, recognizing that civil aircraft used, operated, or employed in interstate, overseas, or foreign air commerce were potential targets for saboteurs, fanatics, and misguided invididuals seeking to retaliate against the United States for real or imagined wrongs, amended Title 18 of the United States Code, Willful Damaging of Aircraft (Act of July 14, 1956, 70 Stat. 538, as amended by Act of October 3, 1961, 75 Stat. 751 and Act of July 7, 1965, 79 Stat. 210). This act stipulates punishment for whomever willfully tries to or brings harm to any aircraft, crew member, or facility used or intended to be used in connection with the operation, loading, or unloading of such aircraft.

In 1961, Congress added to Title IX of the Federal Aviation Act
a number of provisions dealing with crimes committed aboard aircraft.
These included natters dealing with aircraft piracy, interference with
the performance of the duties of a flight crew member, and a number
of crimes of violence such as murder and manslaughter. In 1970, following the ratification of the Tokyo Convention, a number of amendments were made to those provisions to fulfill the United States responsibility to implement the Convention.

Prior to the enactment of these amendments most of the criminal
provisions of Title IX applied to acts committed aboard aircraft in
flight. The 1970 amendments extended and clarified federal jurisdiction over these crimes by establishing the "special aircraft jurisdiction of the United States" to include, while in flight:

1. All civil aircraft of the United States
2. All aircraft of the United States national defense
    forces
3. All other aircraft: (a) within the United States,
    or (b) outisde the United States if the aircraft
    has its next scheduled destination or last point
    of departure in the United States, provided that
    the plane next actually lands in the United States

Also in 1970, responding to the growing aircraft piracy situation, the government, with great publicity, announced the establishment of the 1,500-man sky marshal program. The concept was to provide a federal police officer aboard certain aircraft while in flight
to protect passengers and otherwise deter hijackers. The results of
that program are now well known. It was not effective in halting the
alarming increase in air piracy and was shown to be largely ineffec-
tive because of its lack of emphasis on keeping potential skyjackers
off airplanes. Little more than a year after the sky marshal program
began it was quietly abandoned. The marshals who had been hired were
retired from the sky and took up positions at the nation's major airports to provide a federal law enforcement presence aimed at keeping
would-be sky pirates off airplanes.

Until recently, the airlines and the government had relied pri-

marily upon the so-called "hijacker behavioral profile" to identify
would-be hijackers. Generally, only those passengers conforming to
the behavioral traits contained in the profile have been subjected to
screening by weapons-detecting devices or to personal search.

Additional rules were put into effect to provide in-flight security for passengers and crew (such as the Pilot Compartment Security
Rule requiring locking compartment doors, etc.).

Also, Airport Security, Federal Aviation Regulation (FAR) Part
107 became effective March 18, 1972, and provided certain aviation security standards for operators of airports regularly serving scheduled
air carriers. Although FAR Part 107 was implemented primarily to stop
hijackings it acted as a deterrent to air cargo thefts as well. The
year 1972 still produced 31 attempted hijackings in the United States.
Therfore, the federal government took further action.

On December 5, 1972, after Congress had adjourned and without
prior notice or consultation with Congress or the aviation community,
the Secretary of Transportation called a news conference and announced
emergency regulations to deal with aircraft piracy which were to become effective within 60 days. This was done by amending FAR Part
107. The regulations required airline screening of passengers and
carry-on possessions effective January 5, 1973. The second part of
the regulations required that state and local governments, who own and
operate the nation's 531 airline-served airports, furnish uniformed,
armed law enforcement officers at each passenger screening point beginning February 6, 1973.

The announcement astonished the nation's airport operators, cities, counties and state governments. They had no opportunity to review the proposal, to comment, to testify in public hearings, or to
otherwise participate in the rule-making process. Normal rule-making
procedure, which is provided for under law, was abandoned because of
the emergency which existed at the time, the federal government al-
leged.

The new rules, in effect, make baggage inspection and passenger
screening airline functions, and assign to airport operators the re-

sponsibilities for insuring that at least one law enforcement officer is present at the passenger screening checkpoint prior to and during boarding. During the first six months of 1973 only one hijacking attempt occurred in the United States and it was not completed.

2. International Actions on Security

The first international step to abate the increasing number of hijackings was the Tokyo Convention (Punishment of Offenses Committed on Board Aircraft) held in 1963. The Tokyo Convention provides that the state of registration of the aircraft is competent to exercise jurisdiction over offenses committed on an aircraft. It empowers the aircraft commander to prevent the commission of such acts. In event of unlawful and forcible seizure of an aircraft, it obliges the states that are parties to the convention to take all steps to restore control of the aircraft to the lawful commander or to preserve his control.

Over 38 countries have ratified the Tokyo Convention. It became effective December 4, 1969, but had little or no apparent effect on the number of hijacking attempts. Because the Tokyo Convention does not oblige any state to establish jurisdiction over hijacking, or to extradite or submit to prosecution hijackers in its custody, a gap in the international legal system existed. To close this gap the Hague Convention for the Suppression of Unlawful Seizure of Aircraft was adopted in December 1970. The convention obligates signatory nations to establish jurisdiction over hijackers and agree to extradite or submit to prosecution offenders in its custody. The convention requires each contracting state to establish jurisdiction to punish hijacking and any other act of violence against passengers or aircraft crews committed in connection with the offense when (1) the offense is committed on board an aircraft registered in that state, (2) the aircraft on which the offense is committed lands in that state with the hijacker on board, or (3) the aircraft on which the offense is committed is leased to one whose principal place of business, or permanent residence is in that state. In addition, each contracting state In addition, each contracting state is required, regardless of where the offense is committed, to establish jurisdiction to prosecute any hijacker found within its borders whom it does not extradite. The Hague Convention was signed September 14, 1971 by the United States and went into effect October 14, 1971.

The year 1972 still produced 62 hijackings, 23 of which were successful. One of the major reasons international political hijacking continued unabated was the fact that certain nations encouraged or condoned air piracy by refusing to punish or extradite hijackers who sought sanctuary in their territory. Such nations refused to abide by the provisions of the Hague Convention and apparently still believed that aircraft piracy is a legitimate expression of political or social dissent or an acceptable means of fleeing to political asylum.

Additional steps to deal with the rising wave of aircraft piracy on an international level were being taken by the International Civil Aviation Organization (UCAO) in the form of the Montreal Convention (Convention for the Suppression of Unlawful Acts Against the Safety of Civil Aviation) held in September 1971. It was signed November 1, 1972 and went into effect January 26, 1973. This convention defines various actions (sabotage, bombings, or armed attacks) and declares each to be a severely punishable offense.

3. Cargo Security

While the public's attention and the majority of governmental effort has been focused on and directed toward the hijacking and air piracy problem, organized crime and pilferers have found the theft of air cargo to be a "soft touch." The direct cost of air cargo thefts is estimated to be about $1\frac{1}{2}\%$ of gross revenues and remains a major airport security problem. The indirect costs -- for paperwork, claims process and man-hours -- adds between $2 to $5 to every $1 of direct costs. According to former U.S. Secretary of Transportation, John A. Volpe, "Available statistics (and these must be considered conservative) indicate that transportation-related crime is costing every man, woman and child in our country at least $5.00 a year in higher prices." And Senator Alan Bible, whose U.S. Senate investigation committee first put the public spotlight on the total United States cargo crime problem, believes the aggregate cost to our economy may total $8 billion to $10 billion annually.

In June 1971, DOT Secretary Volpe established the Interagency Committee on Transportation Security, involving 14 government departments and agencies, to perform the following functions:

1. Work with the transportation industry to determine the extent of cargo crime; determine where, when, and how it was being committed; by whom; and the modes and commodities most vulnerable.

2. Develop and recommend corrective actions.

3. Alert industry and aviation leaders that air cargo theft and pilferage can no longer be swept under the rug or shrugged off as just another cost of doing business.

It has been estimated that losses due to air cargo thefts approximated $110 million in 1971 alone, this is about 9% of the provable total of $1.5 billion in goods stolen from all transportation modes that year.

Air cargo thefts are primarily a local problem for the airport, airline, and insurance company. On June 3, 1968, 26 airlines joined the newly formed Airport Security Council for the New York area. The council was formed to develop methods and systems to protect the increasing $3.64 million annual cargo business at the three New York area airports, from the growing losses to theft. The increased tonnage of cargo shipped by air created logistical problems involving the expeditious handling and protection of the growing amounts of freight.

Today, provisions in Title 18 of the United States Code, Embezzlement and Theft (Act of June 25, 1948, 62 Stat. 729, as amended by Act of May 24, 1969, 63 Stat. 91) and the Act of October 14, 1966 (80 Stat. 904) prescribe punishment for any individual who embezzles or steals from any vehicle storage facility, terminal, or pipeline system any goods or chattels moving in interstate or foreign commerce. Adequate penal laws also exist at local and state levels to effectively prosecute those stealing air cargo.

B. CONSTRAINTS

The new FAR 107 has placed the burden of security for airports served by airlines upon the airport manager of each airport, and FAR 121 places the responsibility for the security of the aircraft, including passengers and baggage, upon the air carriers. These security regulations require airlines to electronically screen all passengers and search all carry-on baggage. These regulations also require the nation's public airport operators to station armed local law enforcement officers at passenger checkpoints during periods when passengers are boarding or reboarding their flights.

As far as this order applies to the 531 airports across the United States, the approach to the problem may be correct. The method of outlined by the Department of Transportation, however, is argued by many to be the wrong solution. This based on the fact that air piracy involving political terrorism and extortion is a national and international problem requiring the leadership and resources of the United States Government; and, on an international basis, the ICAO.

1. System Constraints

a. Legal As required in FAR Part 107, local armed security officers must be provided by 531 different local jurisdictions. There will be 531 sets of employment qualifications, 531 different methods of selection, training, and supervision. Part 107 requires only that the law enforcement officer be an armed person authorized to carry and use firearms, vested with proper police power, and identifiable by uniform.

Other problems facing local government involve legal constraints. In various states, perhaps eighteen or twenty, state and local officers have no statutory authority to enforce United States statutes and to make arrests for violations of them.

In many instances, peace officers employed by state and local governments have no statutory authority to arrest without warrant for suspected violation of federal criminal statutes (felony or misdemeanor. This is true, according to Justice Department reports, in the following 19 states, whose air carrier airports enplane a total of some 40% of total domestic passenger traffic:

No jurisdiction over federal felonies	No jurisdiction over federal misdemeanors not committed in officers presence
Connecticut	Georgia
Hawaii	Idaho
Illinois	Ohio
Indiana	Oklahoma
Maine	Tennessee
Massachusetts	Texas
Missouri	Washington
Montana	Wyoming
Nevada	
North Carolina	
Vermont	

b. Economic In addition to the legal problems, a major constraint is economics. It appears that an additional $56.4 million will be required to pay for over 4,000 additional employees required to man passenger screening points at airports. On March 14, 1973, the Civil Aeronautics Board (CAB) authorized the nation's airlines to add 34¢ to the cost of each passenger trip-segment to defray the expense of anti-hijacking airline passenger-baggage screening, but refused to authorize a further increase to pay for salaries of armed guards at airports. On May 4, 1973, the CAB finally approved requests of the carriers for a 25¢ increase to the existing 34¢ surcharge on airline passengers to cover costs of the airport security armed guard program as mandated by FAR Part 107.4.

Responses from management at various United States public airports in an early June 1973 survey indicate that the willingness of the airlines to reimburse the airports for expenses incurred in implementing and maintaining the airport security program is proportional to the size of the airport. The smaller the airport the more difficult it is to get reimbursed by the airlines. The survey also produced the following information. Only 20% and 30% of all responding airports have completed their discussions with carriers for Part 107.4 cost reimbursement, and 59.5% of all responding airports have

begun, but have not completed, their discussions. The responding airports indicate that 62.6% of the large hub airports, 30.8% of the medium, 20.0% of the small, and 4.3% of the non-hubs will be reimbursed
to cover all Part 107.4 costs incurred.

The total unreimbursed costs, based upon the projected averages,
will for large hubs exceed $1,933,051; medium hubs, $1,070,316; small
hubs, $1,307,010; and non-hubs, $1,735,380. These amounts may never
be recovered by the individual airports unless appropriate action is
taken by the CAB.

2. User Constraints

a. Economic. The air traveler is now faced with the additional
fare increase of 59¢ per flight coupon to pay for a system that many
contend should be a federal function.

b. Physical. Today's air traveler is now subject to the additional boarding delay imposed bt the mandatory screening process, the
possibility of embarassment as personal possessions are exposed to
public view, the added exposure to theft of exposed valuables, and the
possibility of false arrest and confiscation of personal property.

C. STATE OF THE TECHNOLOGY

Various devices have been developed and put in use to increase
the level of airport security:

A portable short-pulse x-ray machine combines x-ray and television technology to intensify a faint fluoroscopic image, store
it, and display it on a conventional TV monitor for up to 15 usable minutes. This device is used in an anti-hijacking role to
check carry-on baggage.

Magnometers are used to detect the presence of metal masses
concealed on a person. The metal mass breaks lines of magnetic
flux which register on an indicator providing either a visual
or audio indication.

Closed circuit television systems are installed to monitor
areas for the presence of unauthorized personnel or happenings
of a suspicious nature.

The greatest number of developments occurred in the area of access control. Many ingenious locks have been devised to deny unauthorized entry to restricted airport areas:

Combination locks require either the turning through or aligning of a series of numbers in a given sequence;

Cipher locks require the punching of a series of numbered or lettered buttons in the proper order;

Magnetic locks require that a properly coded card be inserted to gain access either automatically or by requiring the additional activation of a cipher lock. The cards may also be used as photo identity cards or access authorization badges.

Electronic key locks require binary coded keys to release them;

Sequence locks must be locked in sequence for the final lock to function;

Magnetic locks may be operated by a remote switch;

Dual locking cylinders prevent key jiggling, picking, impressioning, or the use of lock aid guns.

Other devices used to control access are the electronic access, warning and control systems. The electronic system powered by an independent power source combines magnetic contact switches, infrared beams, and ultrasonic detectors to provide access warning information. External alarm circuitry may also be included. The external alarm system may include local audio signals or remote signals, and may also include dialers which will call any series of programmed phone numbers.

In addition to the special locks, badges, gates, doors, scanners, and detectors developed to limit access or detect unauthorized entry, additional development has taken place in the area of lighting and the use of lighting. Photoelectric controlled mercury metal halide, or quartz lucalow lamps are now in use to protect previously vulnerable airport areas.

Dogs have been trained to detect explosives and contraband. Electronic sniffers and vapor detectors have been developed for detection of certain odors and specific vapor concentrations, providing warning of potentially dangerous accumulations.

Of all the many security systems, devices and methods developed, one of the most significant is the new security awareness.

PANEL SUMMARY

In reviewing the output of this panel considerable concern is evident in the areas of aircraft and cargo security. Adapting to regulations presented by the federal government and the interaction with the variety of institutions involved in the process has become a complicated picture for local government, the airport operators, and the affected industry.

The basic purpose of the regulations cited in the problem statement were in response to a volunteer program that just did not work; the system unfortunately was not uniformly applied. There now exists 100% screening of all passengers boarding aircraft, as well as uniformed police officers in the boarding area. Since the screening has been put into effect there has not been a successful skyjacking. While there have been several attempts in the terminal boarding area, these were effectively deterred by the presence of law enforcement officers at the airports. The screening of the carry-on luggage has prevented any introduction of weapons or dangerous objects on board. The main purpose of the regulations is to prevent unauthorized entrance to aircraft when they are in the operations area and to prevent passengers from bringing dangerous weapons onto the aircraft.

Airport security is an activity that airport operators have been concerned with for many years. Although maybe not to the degree that they should have been, and not in a manner that was adaptable to current-day airport crimes. So it was inevitable that regulations be put into effect when the crimes had reached the point that airport operators could not handle them. The fact still remains that it is up to the airport operator and the community to adopt a program for each local airport and to put that program into effect. There is no question, from the record itself, that the federal government's programs are working well and are now being carried out. Concerns are shifting to the long-range cost of the program, the ability to staff effectively within each community, and the law enforcement and training programs. As a result, state legislation is being passed establishing peace officer requirements. Furthermore, the education and training process must be ongoing so that as new and better means are developed for this job, the airport officers can stay abreast. Many things have been done by airports in accordance with the direction and guidelines set forth by the federal regulations. The airport operators have reacted as directed. In many ways there are better, less expensive ways of accomplishing security at airports. These must be developed as time goes by, and programs must be adaptable. The airport operators and federal government cannot be frozen into a system of security, security force, or security program that is incapable of adaptation and changes as time goes by.

In terms of the audience's reaction to the problem, a multitude of questions arose. These can be segmented into those concerned with hijacking measures, cargo theft problems, and institution constructs useful for implementing the growing body of regulations.

With regard to the cargo problems, we may observe first that this year air cargo is going to have its first billion dollar revenue year. Statistics show that each quarter of each year the cargo-loss ratio decreases. The cargo-loss ratio for 1972 was 0.97. This means that 97¢ of each $100 of revenue was paid out in claims. These are not only claims for theft, pilferage, or shortage which are called theft-related claims, but also include claims for damage, spoilage, and the like. Theft-related claims account for 55% of that 97¢, with the balance for spoilage, damage, and things of that nature. Fortunately, cargo security systems are improving year by year and in the last two-year period, the ratio has been reduced from $1.68 to $0.97.

Skyjacking and related problems, however, received the greatest attention due to the fact that many in the audience are frequent air travelers and are concerned. In a sense, they transcended their job-related interest. We discuss here the variety of measures instituted to eliminate hijacking and the related costs and equipment.

In relation to ground security measures, it is pertinent first to review the nature of the individual committing the crime of sky-jacking. From a security standpoint, the safety of a sterile concourse system (that is, when passengers are screened in a hall instead of at a gate) adds a lot. Many people have underestimated the security benefit of such a system. Every person committing a crime has to pass a certain threshold. For the embezzler, when he opens the cash register and puts his hand in, that's his threshold. For the burglar, when he is opening the door or going through the window, that's the threshold he has to pass. In the use of the sterile concourse we have interposed a lot of thresholds. The first would be the search of his carry-on luggage; the second, passing by a law enforcement officer; the third, a buffer area unknown to him. He does not know what to expect, and he does not know which planes will be boarding at that time and at what gate. He will not know if the jet-way doors are locked or if the airplane doors are locked. He does not know if there are other police officers there or on their way there on a roving patrol. Hijackers must weigh all this in their minds and may decide to forget it; this may account for all the weapons found in potted plants and waste paper baskets in the public areas. This concept of threshold may be one that has been overlooked but procedures seem to reinforce its utility.

Now let's consider the various ingredients of safety operations. Regarding the parked aircraft, systems for security of parked aircraft exist. There is some technology that can be used for this but more and better technology is needed. For example, most of the parked-air-craft -- anti-intrusion devices are only good for a certain area and that area is only good for the parking of a few planes. In buying a system for protection of those planes, the cost is related not only to the system itself but to the men necessary to operate such a system. Most airlines feel it is cheaper to use a guard because he's needed anyway and can physically watch the planes. The aircraft are also "buttoned up". There are other procedures as well, since it is necessary to make sure that there is no tampering with the airplane while it is parked at night.

Ground security from the standpoint of the airport operator involves installing fences which must be patrolled and guarded to maintain its security posture. One problem that larger airport operators
have is the need for a number of inspections of the perimeter 24 hours
a day. How is this done? Is a manned guardpost established? This is
an increase in personnel cost even for a small airport to handle on a
12-hour basis. In any case, airport operators are securing the perimeter of their airfield as well as the total airside. This includes
photo ID cards that each employee must wear while working on aircraft
or around the field, in the terminal, or in service areas; this includes an I.D. which must be placed on every vehicle on the field.
Airport operators are depending on tried and true security procedures
such as security guards in patrol cars driving around the perimeter
and the airline terminals, maintaining an awareness of who is on the
field or around it.

With regard to large operations, there are about 40 or 50 major
airports in this country. But there are 531 airports in toto; all of
them have the same federal regulations hanging over their heads for
securing their operations. It is the little airport that is getting
hurt by these high security costs. Small airports which have three,
four or five scheduled flights a day must secure their airport operation to the complete satisfaction of the FAA. The cost of security
personnel and of physical improvements are especially high when spread
over so few flights. All airports are looking toward, and have encouraged industry to produce sophisticated and inexpensive devices
which can be adapted civil airport use. Perimeter security that is reliable yet inexpensive is important. For example, a different type
of closed circuit TV with a longer range and more adaptable than the
typical closed circuit TV, anti-intrusion devices, sonic pulses, and
so on are needed. Another requirement is for sensory devices which can
tell whether someone is tunneling under a fence or if someone is attempting to move through the fence by cutting it or pushing it down
with a vehicle. This type of thing is in the mill but has not yet
been adapted for airports. The federal government has denied funds

for such new devices, primarily because acceptable one have yet to be produced. Clearly, there are not many airports, faced with the cost of security personnel, the cost of adapting terminals or operating the airport in other ways to maintain security, which are going to have the money to do the job. There are not many which have the money to invest in 10-to-12-mile perimeter security systems. The FAA turned down an airport in California (Orange County) for an application for closed circuit TV. It appears that the government attitude is not to share the cost of this type of system.

At this juncture, it is important to state the FAA philosophy as pointed out during the panel discussion. Surely they don't plan to make Fort Knox's out of airports. While they realize that airports are there to move passengers and cargo as safely and as quickly as possible, they do feel that the times demand certain levels of security. FAA security regulations require that each airport operator survey his airport and look for security weaknesses, make out a plan in a time-phased manner, and find out how he can secure his airport. The purpose of the program again is to balance security with travel, which is their interpretation of the new regulations.

We now consider the operators of the airport at the time of an emergency. The experiences of the airport security committee at Los Angeles International Airport was used as an example of a viable new institution developed in response to security needs. It works hand-in-hand with federal counterparts so that complete monitoring of such emergencies is available. We first treat the function of the security committee and then the various procedures which are activated both locally and nationally in the event of a skyjacking or other threat.

One of the important problems is maintaining a good security attitude on the part of airport and airline employees, and people moving in and about the terminals and airfield side of the airport. Keeping security uppermost in their mind and intent is a constant problem. The only way the Los Angeles International Airport management felt it could remain sensitive and keep the program sensitive to change, was through the actions of a security committee. Represented on the committee are members of the airlines, the airport operation personnel, and the complete spectrum of law enforcement people at the airport. This committee structure is one way in which the airport security program can stay current, keep attitudes alive, and keep security fresh in everyone's mind. It is also useful for constant evaluation, for changing things that need changing, and for substituting things that aren't working. It also serves as a means to better coordinate efforts when there is a crisis. As a working committee, each member has a better understanding of the other roles, which results in better coordination, since everyone is used to working together through meeting and discussing the response needed for a security crisis. This holds true for airports as small as Scotts Bluff, Nebraska or as large as O'Hare, La Guardia, or Logan.

It is essential that airport operators or municipal officials within a community bring local law enforcement in contact with the airlines so that everyone can understand the problems and become sympathetic to what the airlines are trying to do. The airport committee does an excellent job of accomplishing this.

Such committees are established under the Air Transport Association and exist at the 48 largest airports in the United States. Any information of a security nature which comes into any of the central offices is sent to the chairman of these airport committees who disseminates it to each representative on his committee.

Now, let us track the system as it would apply to an emergency situation. From the national point of view, the one thing that the FAA is trying to stress is that because everyone is excited,they should slow down. The hijacker is at his peak, and for safety's sake everyone should act in a very deliberate fashion. When a hijacking occurs, the pilot will signal the traffic center which has been keeping the aircraft under radar coverage. The com-center in Washington is then called and, in turn, calls the director or his assistant at the FAA. A team is set up in that com-center. A conference call is then arranged to bring in the air traffic facilities controlling the aircraft and to notify the field facilities and airport people; that is, the

FAA tower at Los Angeles, alerted that a hijacked aircraft was coming
into that airport, would activate their security committee. Notifi-
cation is sent to the national military command center and they offer
back-up communication facilities. (The FAA communications center is
second only to the military command center's communications system.)
A vast network of communications exists and if, for example, Cuba is
the destination, the State Department is advised, and they immediately
begin to make arrangements for meeting the airplane when it lands at
its final destination, and to arrange for the recovery of the passengers and crew of the plane. The White House is notified although they
seldom get involved unless there is a request from the hijacker. After this, the highest decision-maker of the airline is brought into
the com-center. The whole purpose of this com-center is indeed communication, so that no one goes off without knowing the full context
of what is happening. At this point, the airlines permit the FAA to
monitor the company frequency and the discussions between the pilot
and his company, as well as the conversations between the pilot and
the FAA air traffic facilities. The FAA game-plans with the airline
and the FBI. Some of the suggestions are relayed to the local area
and to the decision-makers at the airport. Also present in the com-
center are PR people. Because the press is usually the first to cover
the hijacking, the stories and misinformation can be fantastic without PR supervision. Most important and emphasized over and over,
is the necessity for communication with all involved so that no one
places the lives of the passengers and crew in jeopardy.

One of the more difficult situations are bomb threats. Presently, airports average about 100 such threats each month which require
a diversion of the aircraft to make a thorough search. The FAA, in
cooperation with law enforcement agencies, has selected 20 key airports in which x-ray systems and trained dog teams have been set up.
This way, if there is a bomb threat, the plane will be within 20 minutes of an airport which has the requisite equipment to hasten the
search. In addition, the FAA has been working with the phone people
in an effort to work out a method to quickly trace phone calls. It
is felt that with a few arrests the resulting publicity would deter
many of the phone calls.

More studies are being done with experimental detection devices and explosive-sniffing devices. At this moment, dogs are particularly favored for sniffing.

Now consider what happens locally when the FAA alerts the tower at Los Angeles Airport. Procedures in effect there have been worked out through the airport security committee's efforts. The airline's phone circuits are used for communications and once having received an alert from local police, FBI or a direct phone call, and if it has attained a status of positive identification, an alert phase is initiated. A system which puts a notice into every airlines operation office is used. (There are some 39 airlines at the Los Angeles airport.) The airlines then respond at the level or degree of involvement required. If it is a general alert, they crank up their security; if it is a specific alert involving an inbound aircraft arriving at the airport, the committee goes into its command-post procedure and moves to a particular building at the airport where there are extensive telephone communications. A controller from the FAA tower joins the committee; he can control the aircraft once it lands. There are three rooms where tables are set up with each representative's nameplate by his telephone. In roughly 20 minutes everything is in operation.

The FAA people from security and the regional office join them. The airline involved is represented at the scene, if possible, by an officer who can make policy decisions. A tactical force controls the traffic in and around the airport, and PR people from the airline and airport are there.

The next phase is to monitor the circumstances and the aircraft. Radio communication is monitored through the FAA center and the aircraft can be followed into the airport. The FBI takes over when the aircraft lands, although a representative from the involved airline stands by to determine what course of action, if any, to take when the plane is on the ground. A number of attempts are made to de-escalate the situation and to try to get the passengers off the plane. In the decision room, they decide what to do with the aircraft and those involved. The cheif pilot is also there to share his knowledge of the particular aircraft involved. Needless to say, there is a lot of drama attached. Many of the intermediate and detailed procedures have not been described here, but, by and large, this same sort of operation occurs at every airport in the event of an emergency.

The problem of cost, as noted above, is of crucial importance to the whole security operation. The theory is that the passenger using the system should pay for it. The CAB permitted a surcharge on each flight segment to be directed to the airline's cost of screening and 25¢ for the cost of the uniformed police officer supplied by the airport. The airport has the responsibility of the police officer, and the airline the responsibility for the screening. Physical improvement costs are shared under the Airport Development Act. The FAA is now permitted to provide 82% of the cost of such things as airport fencing and similar security expenses. This is managed by the Airport Service of FAA which examines and evaluates the allocation of the funds as to whether or not it is necessary for security measures. It is hoped that this federal participation will be expanded to all airport security costs for physical items. An amendment to Part 107 is being prepared which will clearly spell out what will be eligible for the 82%. This has not yet reached the policy discussion level; it is one of the items to be covered.

However, if it had not been for this federal program and these regulations, airports would not have achieved the level of security they have today. What about the future? Fortunately, the FAA attitude has been one the industry can live with. If it had been overly dictatorial, it may have caused deep trouble. The passengers, especially the frequent travelers, would have been affected adversely to a greater degree than the airline or the airport operator. The airlines do feel it in the pocketbook but the airport operator is caught in between, unable to easily do what the government is demanding. In the future, the technology will probably revert to systems produced by industry. Hopefully, new products and devices can be adapted to strengthen airport security.

II. BUS TRANSPORTATION SYSTEMS

FRED B. BURKE

Public Technology, Inc.
Washington, D.C.

PROBLEM STATEMENT

Expose and discuss innovations in bus transportation as one method for improving local mass transit.

A. INTRODUCTION

The nation's urban bus systems are in a crisis. In most urban areas transit patronage today is less than three-quarters of what it was 15 years ago and a third of what it was 25 years ago.

Bus operations in our urban areas have long been dominated by private operators who were able to make a profit on their operations. Local governments over the last decades have learned that this is no longer the way of life, with community after community faced with the option of taking over the private bus operation or going without public transportation. With the takeover has come the reality of the need for some form of subsidy to cover, along with the fare box revenues, total operating costs. In 1966, 26 local transit systems were subsidized and in 1972, 150 were in existence.

More and more it is recognized that public policy should be aimed toward substantially increasing ridership, and thus produce a more balanced transportation system in our nation's urban areas. Public policy, in the past, has forced the automobile on public transportation. But, if the simple existence of more cars is not used to justify more and more highways, with the accompanying problems of pollution and congestion, ecological destruction, higher relocation costs, and unwise land use, mass transit will have to become a viable alternative.

The 1970 Urban Transportation Act and the 1973 Federal Aid Highway act make major strides in turning about federal policy. Actions by many of the states do the same. Efforts in Washington to obtain larger amounts of federal aid for capital investments for transit aid will also continue.

But what can be done within the framework of the present capital structure of transit systems or with relatively small investments to attract more riders or improve the financial picture of transit systems? This clearly calls for advances to made in technology.

Certainly, a 15-year-old, poorly maintained bus sitting in the middle of a traffic jam on an urban expressway is not an attractive alternative to the automobile. The management of streets and traffic so that priority is given to the bus is one way to improve this situation.

In less dense areas, bus service can appropriately be limited to one every half hour or hour. Waiting those lengths of time in inclement weather, however, can force the most ardent advocate of ecology to seek an automobile. Experience with demand responsive transit systems has provided some excellent examples of how to improve bus service.

Obviously, private and public bus operations which are slowly bleeding to death financially are not always able to provide the most up-to-date systems of maintenance, management, and bus scheduling. These require the analysis of considerable amounts of data to efficiently carry out their objectives. However, little use has been made of computers.

These three areas -- priority treatment for buses, demand responsive transit systems, and assistance to bus management through computers -- are the topics discussed in the following presentations. This modus operandi differed in some respects from that used in other working groups. Here our purpose was to put before the panel methods already existing but requiring application on a wide basis for ultimate success.

The description of priority treatment for buses was prepared by Ronald J. Fisher of the Office of Transit Planning of the Urban Mass Transportation Administration (UMTA). Both UMTA and the Federal Highway Administration have been active in supporting these programs. Mr. Fisher directed UMTA's efforts in this very vital area.

The discussion on demand responsive transit systems was prepared by Robert S. Scott and Arthur Schwartz of Chase, Rosen & Wallace, Inc. Both Mr. Scott and Mr. Schwartz have been involved in the development of some of the demand responsive projects. In addition, they have also surveyed several other programs in preparation for their comments.

The presentation on the use of computers to assist in transit management was prepared by Costis Toregas of Public Technology, Inc.

B.   PRIORITY TREATMENT FOR BUSES

The UMTA and the Federal Highway Administration have been actively involved in programs to improve bus operations in congested urban areas.   These improvements are being implemented at the local level. They usually involve a cooperative effort by city traffic engineering departments, public transit agencies, and the State Highway Department acting in concert with a mixture of federal programs for fund support.

The impact of the effort is directed toward accomplishing these objectives:

Diverting auto commuters to transit

Improving the transit system performance, that is, lowering unit costs, increasing speeds, improving reliability

Reducing air pollutants

Reducing fuel consumption

For example, in northern Virginia the Shirley Highway Express Bus Demonstration is now diverting 7,000 northern Virginia auto commuters each weekday. It is estimated that 4,000 fewer automobiles are now traveling the streets and highways in that urban corridor each peak period. This translates into a reduction of 12 tons of air pollutants and 7,000 gallons of gasoline each weekday.   The techniques for accomplishing these bus priority improvements include giving buses priority entry to freeways, priority at traffic signals, reserving lanes on city streets and highways, both in the direction of traffic and counter to the flow of traffic, and finally the most expensive -- exclusive bus facilities. Projects to demonstrate these techniques are either in operation or in the process of being implemented in the locations noted. A brief description and the recent status of these projects follow.

1.   Exclusive Bus Lanes

A lane of freeway can be physically separated from other lanes either in the median or on adjacent right-of-way, and made available for the exclusive use of buses in corridors of existing high bus usage, or in areas planned for such high usage. The facility itself will help provide demand for the service; current bus usage should not be used as the only criterion for establishment of the facility. However, because of the comparatively high cost of these exclusive bus lanes (for example, upwards of $5,000 per mile for the San Bernardino Busway in California), significantly greater bus volumes must be involved than with any other bus priority technique.

Perhaps the best known exclusive bus lane in the United States is on Shirley Highway (I-95) in northern Virginia. Plans for preferential treatment of buses on Shirley Highway had been under discussion since 1964. In September 1969, buses were allowed to use a portion of the completed reversible roadway on I-95 to bypass traffic queues. Ridership at that time was about 1,900 passengers on 39 buses in the morning peak period. Since that time, project ridership on this same portion of the roadway has grown to over 9,700 passengers on 200 buses in the morning peak period. The bus roadway is also used by other transit buses and private commuter carriers over portions of its 11-mile length, bringing the total morning peak period utilization to over 17,000 passengers on more than 370 buses. This represents an attraction of about 7,000 new transit riders and a diversion of 4,000 automobiles from highways during the morning peak period. During the combined morning and afternoon peak periods over 33,000 passengers realize time savings over part or all of the bus roadway.

Recently, a reconstructed section on Shirley Highway was opened to traffic. As a result, automobile travel times were cut in half and the number of cars crossing the project screenline doubled. Auto volume during the 6:30 to 9:00 a.m. peak period went from 6,416 in March 1973 to 11,392 in June 1973. Thus far, bus ridership has not been affected; in fact, it is still climbing and overcrowding is still a problem. Continued efforts to expand the service will be made by the Washington Metropolitan Area Transit Authority which plans to put an additional 50 buses in service on Shirley Highway in the coming year.

The Shirley Highway reconstruction is due to be completed in August 1975. The reversible roadway averaged over $10,000 per mile to construct in northern Virginia. Present plans call for the use of the completed reversible roadway by buses and carpools with four or more occupants.

The first freeway lane to be designed and built exclusively for buses is on the San Bernardino Freeway in Los Angeles. This busway will extend 11.2 miles from El Monte to downtown Los Angeles. This facility provides rapid transit service using exclusive bus lanes. There will be three stations along the route including a major facility at El Monte, and smaller stations at the California State University and near the County Medical Center.

The first stage, 6.6 miles long, was opened on January 27, 1973. This section has a 17-foot lane located on each side of a railroad line in the median of the freeway. It is separated from the railroad by a concrete barrier and from the freeway by plastic traffic posts and a 10-foot shoulder. Before the opening of the first stage, ridership during the combined morning and afternoon peak periods was about 1,000 passengers.

The El Monte Terminal was opened on July 15, 1973. This facility can accommodate 700 automobiles and there are plans for future expansion to 1,400 spaces. During the morning peak period, buses leave on a three-minute headway. Base period headways are 10 minutes. With this opening, service has increased considerably and ridership has already climbed to over 2,000 passengers.

Stage two of the $53 million project is scheduled to be completed
in June 1974. This section will be adjacent to the freeway right-of-
way. The busway will have two 12-foot lanes with 8-foot interiors and
4-foot exterior shoulders. The lanes will be separated by a concrete
barrier. The future estimated passenger volume for the entire busway
is 17,000 two-way passengers per day with 10,000 of these utilizing
the El Monte terminal. The current nine-minute time savings will be
increased to about fifteen minutes. The buses will travel at 40 mph
during the trip into Los Angeles. The fare from El Monte is 70¢.

2.   Express Bus on Freeway: Mixed Traffic with Priority Treatment

On many freeways traffic congestion is not yet a major problem
and buses can cover the line-haul portion of the trip in mixed traffic as quickly as on an exclusive bus lane. In these cases the efficiency of the facility can be improved in terms of the number of people carried during peak periods by attracting automobile drivers to
improved express transit service. These improvements include shorter
headway, more direct express bus service, and construction of park-
ride facilities near the freeway. To preserve the quality of the bus
service during inclement weather and at times when there are traffic
incidents, consideration should be given to priority treatment for
buses at entrances and downtown exits to the freeway. Also, entry of
automobiles onto the freeway can be controlled to optimize traffic
flow under varying traffic conditions on the freeway.

The following includes one example in which buses operate on an
uncongested facility and another where congestion is contained under
most conditions by controlling vehicle access to the freeway.

The Seattle Blue Streak is an express bus operation serving a
suburban area north of Seattle's Central Business District (CBD). The
service provides local collection and distribution and serves a major
park-ride lot near I-5 about seven miles from downtown. The express
buses operate in mixed traffic on I-5 but are provided with an exclusive on-off ramp into the CBD.

The project was successful from its very beginning in September
1970. Three thousand new daily bus riders were attracted to the ser-

vice and the park-ride lot was filled to capacity every day. Service from the lot is provided on a four-minute headway at a fare of 35¢.

The Blue Streak service was influential in the passage of a referendum to increase the sales tax in King County to support transit. An areawide express bus service is planned with increased local and off-peak service. Future plans also call for the establishment of 25 park-ride lots, exclusive bus counterflow lanes in the CBD and an experimental free bus ride area in the CBD starting in September 1973.

A metered freeway system is currently being installed in the corridor south of Minneapolis. Automobiles will be metered onto I-35W at the entrance ramps so that the freeway will not become congested under most conditions. In addition, exclusive bus ramps are being constructed to allow express buses to bypass traffic queues and enter the freeway ahead of other vehicles. Park-ride space has been leased at 13 locations along the corridor. Installation of metering equipment is scheduled for completion by late 1973.

In advance of this, express bus service was started on December 11, 1972 to compare patronage response and system performance before and after the freeway metering. The original 87 inbound trips have now been increased to 96 because of increased ridership. Although the buses currently receive no priority treatment, the service is extremely popular and indicates a strong demand for direct express service to and from the Minneapolis CBD.

3.   Contraflow Bus Lanes on Freeways

Highway facilities often have a directional imbalance in traffic flow during peak periods so that one or even two lanes in the off-peak direction (contraflow) can be reserved for buses.

This approach offers a low capital cost improvement in the efficiency of existing freeways and the possible elimination or deferment of the need to expand existing freeways. Although a recurring maintenance and operating cost is involved in setting up the contraflow operation, it is small compared to other alternatives for expanding the people-moving capacity of the facility. While preliminary concerns about the safety of such an operation have greatly retarded the application of contraflow lanes, actual experience is proving contraflow operation to be as safe as other bus operations.

The first major contraflow bus lane on a limited access highway was established on I-495 in northern New Jersey in December 1970. The lane extends two and a half miles from the New Jersey Turnpike to the Lincoln Tunnel. During the morning peak hours, the outbound median lane is made available to inbound buses. No provision has been made for a contraflow lane in the evening because the traffic flow is not congested outbound from the Lincoln Tunnel. Morning traffic is guided in the use of the contraflow lanes by 80 directional signals placed directly over the outbound lanes, traffic posts placed every 40 feet to designate the contraflow lane, and 50 changeable message signs. Over 950 buses carrying approximately 35,000 commuters (21,000 of them are carried in the peak hour on 485 buses) are now saving an average of 15 minutes each. The buses on the contraflow lanes complete the former 25-minute ride in 10 minutes. Surveys show that 82% of the people riding through the tunnel during the morning peak hour are being carried by bus. Inbound vehicle flow increased 40% during the morning peak period with no adverse effect on outbound flow. Inbound truck and automobile speeds increased and the time all vehicles spent on I-495 was decreased by 23%.

A contraflow bus lane on the Southeast Expressway in Boston was put into operation in May 1971. The $8\frac{1}{2}$ mile bus lane was in operation from 7:00 to 9:00 a.m. and 4:00 to 7:00 p.m. There were 80 buses using the lane, carrying 3,500 passengers during each peak period. In the first two years of operation, bus passengers increased 16%, 350 new passengers in the morning peak period. Bus patrons were saving up to 15 minutes in travel time.

The project received favorable press coverage but was discontinued in October 1971 for the winter. Decreasing hours of daylight, and snow and ice conditions in the winter months caused concern for the safety of crews setting traffic cones on this unlighted freeway. The exclusive bus lane operation was resumed from April to November 1972,

and again in April 1973 for the morning rush hours only. The deletion
of the afternoon operation (time savings of only five minutes) was
was made because of an unfavorable cost-benefit ration.

This bus lane was closed recently after an accident in the lane.
The work crew had finished placing the bus lane delineators and were
waiting in the holding area when they were struck by a passing truck.
It is not known whether it will be reopened.

On the Long Island Expressway in New York City, a contraflow bus
lane for Manhattan-bound buses was set up in October 1971 during the
morning rush hours. The project is located on the two miles of expressway from the Brooklyn-Queens Expressway to the Queens-Midtown
Tunnel. Over 200 buses are being directed through a cut in the median barrier onto the special lane. These buses, carrying about 9,500
people, average $3\frac{1}{2}$ minutes on the 2 miles to the tunnel. Vehicles
traveling the same distance in the three westbound regular lanes average 18 minutes. Traffic in the remaining eastbound lanes is not delayed despite the loss of a lane.

A contraflow bus lane in the San Francisco area was implemented
in September 1972 on Route 101, north of the Golden Gate Bridge. The
5-mile lane operates in the evening peak period. An 80-20 directional
split of traffic permits the closing of two of the four lanes in the
non-peak direction without delaying traffic there. One of the closed
lanes acts as a buffer between opposing directions of travel. The
Golden Gate Bridge District has been providing expanded bus service
in this corridor since January 1972. Before the Golden Gate Bridge
District took over the operation of the bus service from Greyhound,
approximately 4,100 passengers journeyed by bus to work in San Francisco across the Golden Gate Bridge. That figure increased 50% to
around 6,000 after the new and expanded bus service was in use a few
months. The number of bus commuters continued to rise and reached
6,700 when the contraflow lane was inaugurated in September 1972. By
August, 1973, ridership had climbed to 7,789 passengers during the 6:00-
to 10:00 a.m.-period with 5,263 passengers crossing the bridge during
the peak hour.

Under normal operating conditions, buses save five minutes by using the contraflow lane. However, time savings of up to 20 minutes
are not unusual when an incident occurs in the regular traffic lanes.
There have been no accidents on the contraflow lane.

Further increases in ridership are now being constrained by lack
of capacity. Plans are being made for the addition of equipment in
the near future.

4. Contraflow Bus Lanes on Arterials

Contraflow bus lanes have been used effectively on arterials and
CBD streets. They facilitate bus movement through congested areas in
or near downtown. They are generally established in conjunction with
a one-way street system which gives them the advantage of being self-
enforcing. Also, buses are not delayed by right-turning traffic as
they often are on a reserved curb lane in the direction of traffic.

Short sections of contraflow bus lanes have been in use for years
in Chicago and in Harrisburg, Pennsylvania. Longer routes have more
recently become operational in San Juan, Indianapolis, and Madison,
Wisconsin. In San Juan, buses save about 25 minutes on the 5.9-mile
contraflow lane on Avinida Ponce de Leon.

Although no comprehensive data are yet available, the opinion of
transportation engineers involved with these projects is that the operation is as safe or safer than the operation of buses on any two-
way street. Contraflow operations do require careful attention to
lane markings and signs directing motorists and pedestrians who would
not otherwise expect to see vehicles coming from the contraflow direction.

5. Traffic Signal Preemption

One of the items in the UMTA demonstration program is an evaluation of the benefits and possible disbenefits to auto traffic in al-
lowing buses to preempt traffic signals. Traffic preemption is in
the process of being tested on line-haul express bus runs on arterial
streets and on bus collection and distribution operations on downtown
street networks. Preemption is being accomplished through two basic

approaches. One involves a computer controlled traffic signal system. The other approach is a direct over-ride of the local controller for the traffic signal on an intersection by intersection basis.

A demonstration of the latter approach is under way in Miami, Florida. Express buses will operate from a park-ride lot at the Golden Glades Interchange north of Miami along NW 7th Avenue into the Miami CBD, Civic Center, and Miami Airport. The line-haul distance along NW 7th Avenue is nine miles. There will be traffic signal preemption at 36 intersections. The buses will operate under several types of traffic signal settings. They will be both progressively timed and non-progressively timed with and without signal preemption. The buses will also be given reserved lanes at the approaches to intersections to allow them to bypass any queues that are present.

The 18-month demonstration project will evaluate the effect of signal preemption on transit service, patronage, traffic flow along NW 7th Avenue and cross streets. The reliability of the preemption equipment and operational safety of the system will also be evaluated.

In Washington, D.C., a computerized traffic signal control system has been implemented with the capability of providing for signal preemption by buses. Computers control 111 intersections in the CBD and 34 intersections are equipped to provide bus preemption of traffic signals; 450 buses are equipped with signal preemption equipment.

However, under this computerized traffic signal system approach, the priority for the bus is subverted to the overall traffic demand on the street system. A bus driver may request additional green time (up to 10 seconds) or shorten the red phase by pressing a button which transmits a signal to a detector buried in the roadway approaching The intersection. The signal is relayed to the computer which decides whether or not to grant additional green time based upon traffic conditions in the direction he is traveling, and on cross streets.

The evaluation here will seek to determine the same types of information as in Miami; the two projects will thus allow a comparison of two different approaches to providing traffic signal preemption.

6. Bus Priority at Toll Plazas

Any location where traffic queues form on a regular basis is a good candidate for some kind of bus priority treatment. In addition to street intersections and freeway on-ramps, toll plazas generally cause traffic backups in peak periods. Giving priority to buses and carpools at these points is usually easy to implement and inexpensive.

The San Francisco Bay Area provided the setting for the first application of this technique. On April 15, 1970, a morning peak period bus lane was reserved in the toll plaza area of the Oakland Bay Bridge. The bus toll was reduced from $1.00 to 65¢ with the buses not stopping to pay the toll (monthly bills were sent to the bus companies). The one-half mile reserved bus lane operation saves five minutes in travel time for patrons of the 500 buses using the bridge during the two-hour peak period.

Later, the University of California and the California Division of Bay Toll Crossings analyzed different plans for bus and carpool lanes in the toll plaza area and on the bridge proper. They developed a plan which was implemented on December 8, 1971. The plan included (1) extended reserved lanes on both sides of the toll plaza, (2) three reserved toll booths, (3) the addition of carpools with three or more occupants to the reserved lanes, and (4) the elimination of tolls for carpools in the reserved lanes.

Results of surveys show that in the morning peak period (1) the automobile occupancy increased from 1.33 to 1.44 persons per automobile; (2) the bus ridership was virtually unaffected; and (3) while the number of vehicles did not significantly change, 2,350 more people were carried in them during the morning peak period.

The existing toll-free structure for carpools during the morning rush has now been changed to a minimal charge of $1.00 a month per carpool. Carpools without the monthly pass may use the special lanes but pay the normal toll. This change was instituted because of a provision in the original bondholder agreements that no vehicles would cross toll free.

Traffic signals to meter traffic downstream from the bridge toll plaza will be in operation by the end of September 1973. During peak hours, the signals will give continuous green to the priority lane buses and carpools after they pass the 17-lane toll plaza where traffic has to merge onto the five lanes of the bridge. During off-peak hours, the signals can be controlled manually to give preference to emergency vehicles or to reroute traffic around accidents and other traffic tieups. A survey on January 10, 1973 found 1,620 carpools using the priority lanes, over 80% of them with monthly carpool passes.

Bus priority treatment is also provided at the toll plaza of the George Washington Bridge in New York City. The 1 mile long reserved bus lane is operated during the morning peak period and time savings of eight to ten minutes are effected for buses.

A bus priority lane was established on September 5, 1973 on the approach to the Evergreen Point Bridge toll plaza in Seattle, Washington. The 1 mile long lane was formed on the paved shoulder of the highway leading to the bridge. It is only open to buses during the morning peak hours and closed to all traffic at other times. The lane is separated by a double yellow line and identified by signs along the side of the road. The time savings for transit users is about five minutes. The entire project was planned and implemented in three months through cooperative efforts of the State of Washington Highway Department and the Seattle Metro Transit System.

7.   Reserved Lanes for Buses and Carpools

Carpools are gaining increased attention as an efficient means of moving people in urban areas. It is generally felt that carpools may complement transit service by serving those trip patterns that are not efficiently served by mass transit; for example, the low density area around the fringe of a metropolitan area.

The opportunity to provide priority treatment for buses is greatly expanded if carpools are also considered. There are many travel corridors where the volume of buses is presently too low to justify a reserved lane of an expensive freeway for buses only. However, the inclusion of carpools would justify reserving the lane. It could be a first step toward developing sufficient bus volume to justify reserving a lane just for buses as more people become attracted to the improved bus service.

Progress on this technique has been retarded by the apparent enforcement problem. Rather limited applications of the technique have been made to date like the preceding example of the reserved bus-carpool lane approaching the San Francisco-Oakland Bay Bridge.

However, firm plans have been made to use this technique as a second phase of the Miami traffic signal preemption demonstration discussed previously. One lane of the I-95 Freeway in the peak direction will be reserved for buses and carpools. An additional lane in each direction will be added to a portion of I-95 north of Miami during the implementation and operation of the traffic signal preemption demonstration. The line-haul bus service will be shifted to the freeway when the lanes are completed. These lanes will be available to buses and carpools only during the peak rush hours.

In addition to evaluating the problems of enforcement, the demonstration will analyze the competitive position of the bus service relative to the carpools. The net effect on reducing vehicle miles of travel from these combined strategies will be reported.

C. DEMAND RESPONSIVE TRANSIT SYSTEMS

1. Description and Rationale

All transit service is to some extent demand responsive. For example, with very few exceptions, the same level of service is not provided at 2:00 a.m. as at 5:00 p.m. However, demand responsive transit systems are defined as those systems in which the routings and schedulings of the vehicle are responsive to demand on a real time basis.

Such systems can take many forms. The so-called "personal rapid transit" systems that have been proposed in several cities are demand

responsive systems operating on exclusive guideways and thus not providing door-to-door service. At the other end of the spectrum, the
ubiquitous taxicab is perhaps the ultimate in demand responsive service. If this reference seems trivial, it should be pointed out that
in a very large number of communities the taxicab is the only public
transportation service.

The class of system which is more specifically referred to in
this section is the demand responsive bus system. This includes all
bus services that provide some form of door-to-door service and are
not constrained to any fixed route. Both fixed-schedule and demand-
schedule services are included since the boundary between these services and a taxi service is difficult to establish. In general, services in this category are designed to serve multiple origins or des-
tinations on the same vehicle trip. Moreover, vehicles larger than
the typical passenger car are commonly used.

The idea of demand responsive transit service is not new, but has
received considerable attention in recent years. The decline in transit usage has forced almost all transit operations to respond by reducing frequency and combining routes. As a result, in all but the
denser areas of the largest cities, it is common to find infrequent
service as well as circuitous routings with large loops and deviations
designed to maximize coverage with a minimum of routes. This level
of service is such that even a trip requiring only one vehicle is often an exercise in delay and frustration while a trip requiring the
use of more than one vehicle may require the expenditure of several
hours.

Unsatisfactory service has resulted in a further decline in usage. In many cities the sole users are those people who have no alternative for transportation. In many of the smaller communities,
this minimal level of usage is not enough to support any transit service and in a number of smaller cities there is no transit service
whatsoever.

Demand responsive transit service has evolved largely as a result of the situations mentioned above. By serving specific demands

rather than areas, transit service can be provided to areas with demand densities which make fixed route service impractical or unattrac-
tive to the user.

Thus, one of the primary roles of demand responsive transit is
that of providing service to the non-automobile user in areas where
fixed route service is impractical. In addition, it is capable of
providing a higher quality of transit service in areas where a marginal level of fixed route service is in operation.

A potential use for demand responsive service is in the replacement of fixed route service during times of the day when the latter
is unsatisfactory. For example, in many cities service is provided
in the evening hours and on weekends for a small number of users. In
such situations, it is likely that a demand responsive system would
be more effective at the same cost.

The higher quality of service provided by demand responsive systems tends to make this type of transit service more competitive with
the automobile. While any transit service using the street system
cannot equal auto travel time and convenience, there is a substantial
segment of the travel market who would be better served by a demand
responsive system which is more convenient than a typical fixed route
bus system.

This segment of the travel market includes those making trips to
areas where parking is limited or costly or beyond walking distance
of a given destination. This situation exists at some suburban railroad stations, industrial complexes, and universities. Another segment of the potential market for demand responsive service are non-
drivers or drivers who do not have exclusive use of a car. Closely
related are trips which are not currently being made because a satisfactory means of travel is not available to this market. The extent
and characteristics of travel potential are difficult to predict.

A specialized form of demand responsive transit service is that
designed to benefit the elderly and the handicapped, who have an over-
riding need for door-to-door service. However, these people tend to

be less sensitive to lengthy travel time than the general population. It has been found that it is difficult to provide the personalized service needed by this group in combination with service to the general population. Such service includes longer boarding time and often assistance in boarding and leaving the vehicle. Provision of a specialized service for the handicapped and elderly would relieve the general transit services from attempting to tackle this problem.

2. A Survey of Existing Operations

In a recent survey, information was collected from nine demand responsive transit systems. Each system was made up of the same components:

A commuter who, hoping to avoid the expense and/or the hassles of using a car, has dialed for a bus to pick him up at his front door.

A sometimes harried dispatcher who receives the call, determines where the passenger is located and where he is destined, and then contacts the bus driver.

The bus driver who receives his instructions, makes his way through traffic to the passenger's house, collects the fare and then pushes on to the destination.

A summary of these systems is offered in Table 1. This information will prove useful, in time, as more data become available for comparison purposes.

In Batavia, New York, the Batavia Dial-a-Bus (known locally as the "B-Line") is one of the few systems making money. In June 1973, a profit of $4,000 was reported. The system carries 1,200 to 2,000 riders per week and charges 60¢ a ride. The B-Line is the only public transportation available to Batavia's 17,000 residents. It has been in service for two years and operates with two Flexette buses which hold 19 riders each.

The Batavia people seem to have sounded out a good market; they provide delivery service, home-to-work subscription service, a special service to Sylvania (the town's largest employer), and home-to-school service for students who don't live near the school bus routes. The buses run from early morning to 6:00 p.m.

TABLE 1

Characteristics of 9 Demand Responsive Systems

	Area (Sq.Mi.)	Population	Riders	Vehicles (Seats)	Fares	Subsidy	Comments
Batavia, New York		17,000	1200-2000/ week	2 Flexettes (19)	60¢	Profit of $4000 (June)	Delivery service work trips (Sylvania) school trips
Greece, New York	10	30,000	714 first week,1141 last week	7 twin coaches (25)	$1.00		Work trips (Kodak), school trips, 2 free phones in retail areas,may promote group fares
Ann Arbor, Michigan	7	3,000 households	400/day	Ford & Dodge Vans (12)	25¢	50% or $225,000/ year	Users largely upper-middle income, $10 monthly pass, will enlarge system with $1,500,000 property tax
Haddonfield, New Jersey	11		21,000/ month	12 twin coaches (17)	60¢		UMTA demonstration, 15 minute service

Location				Vehicles	Fare	Subsidy	Notes
Columbia, Maryland			70-80/day	Ford vans (10)	50¢		Subscription only during rush hours, 15 minute service, Columbia recreation subsidizes
Toronto, Ontario	4	15,000	775/day	Ford Eco'line (11) 1 European Bus (23)	30¢ or 10 for $2.50	$40,000/year	Rail feeder services during rush hours, hour notice for calls
Regina, Saskatchawan	5/ 7½/ 9		2000/day	Chrysler vans (14) Flexette (23)	35¢	30%	City subsidizes, users largely from high income groups
Columbus, Ohio	2½		450/day	5 Flexettes (19)	25¢		
La Habre, California	6½		9000/month	6 Minibuses (19)	50¢	80%	County subsidizes, users largely non-auto owners

PERT Dial-a-Bus services Rochester, New York, and a 10-square mile area known as Greece, New York. The system is referred to as PERT which stands for Personal Transit. It services the 30,000 people living in Greece of whom 7,000 work at Eastman Kodak. Seven twin coaches and twenty-five passenger buses are in operation. PERT is primarily geared toward providing transportation for Kodak employees. Presently, it is used by 500 employees on a home-to-work basis. According to reports, 98% of these riders formerly drove autos to work.

Fifty children are taken to school and an additional twenty are transported to school bus lines on this system. In addition, five large shopping centers are serviced; the local merchants association has installed free Dial-a-Bus phones in two of the centers.

In its first year of operation, PERT's ridership has increased from 714 riders the first week to 1,141. PERT is hoping to promote group ridership which means that the first person of a group going in the same direction pays the usual one-way fare of $1.00, while the rest pay only 25¢ each. Needless to say, this type of plan would appeal to the area's 5,000 senior citizens.

PERT uses digital communications to provide the bus driver with a print-out of the passenger's name, location and destination; a system which had been researched at MIT. Aside from some minor bugs, everything is reported to be running smoothly.

The Dial-a-Bus in Ann Arbor, Michigan services seven square miles containing 3,000 households. Approximately 400 riders are transported daily on Ford and Dodge vans which are equipped to hold twelve passengers each. The Transit Authority is looking for a different type of vehicle, however, which could maneuver driveways with more ease.

The area in Ann Arbor serviced by Dial-a-Bus is characteristic of the rest of the city. There are high-density apartments, seven schools, two shopping centers, two universities, and two hospitals; the last two are also serviced on a fixed-route basis.

It is reported that the upper middle class neighborhood uses the Dial-a-Bus system to a larger extent than others. One-way fare is 25¢.

There is a $10.00 personal pass good for one month of unlimited rides; also a $10.00 family pass is available which is good for one month between the hours of 9:00 a.m. and 3:00 p.m.

After two years, ridership is still increasing. However, fares cover only half of the operating expenses. The city picks up the remaining $225,000 in expenses each year. The citizens of Ann Arbor recently voted to increase their property taxes to fund an expanded demand-response system called "Tel-Tran" which will cost an estimated $1.5 million.

The Haddonfield, New Jersey system services an 11-square mile area and transports 21,000 riders per month. The program, funded by UMTA as a demonstration project, is in operation 24 hours a day, 7 days a week. Service was crippled from March to May 1973 because of a drivers' strike. Director Warren Moore, reports that things are back to normal and a passenger can be picked up within 15 minutes after calling the dispatcher and that ridership is increasing. The radio dispatched buses charge 60¢ per ride and book tickets are also available.

Columbia, Maryland's Call-a-Ride uses 10-passenger Ford Courrier vans to service its runs of $4\frac{1}{2}$ miles. Service during the morning rush hour is on a subscription only basis. The morning runs are made up by the dispatcher the night before. After the rush hours, service is provided on a call basis, with a 10-to-15-minute wait. Approximately 70 to 80 riders use the system daily, each paying 50¢ for a one-way trip. Call-a-Ride is partially funded by Columbia Association's recreational fees.

The Bay Ridge area of Toronto, Canada is serviced by Go-Transit which uses Ford E-200 Econolines seating 11, and one 23-seat European touring bus. The area covered is 4 square miles with a population of 15,000 of whom 775 use the system daily. Ridership has grown at the rate of 4% per week since the system was instituted in July 1970. The service operates from 5:00 a.m. to 1:00 a.m.

A feeder service is provided every 20 minutes during rush hour, with four hundred people using it each day. For pick-up service, a

one hour notice is requested, although pick-ups sometimes are made on
ten minutes notice. A one-way fare costs 30¢; 10 tickets may be purchased for $2.50. The government subsidizes 75% of the equipment costs
and 50% of the operating deficit since fares only cover half of the
costs. For the first year of operation, a deficit of $40,000 was re-
ported.

In Regina, Saskatchewan, Canada, a fleet of 14-passenger Chrys-
ler vans and a 23-passenger Flexette bus services 2,000 riders daily.
However, General Manager Jim McCadoo stated that they are not happy
with the design and performance of the vehicles. The system covers
5 square miles during rush hours, 7½ miles during off-peak hours, and
9 square miles at night. Service is available until midnight, Monday
through Friday.

The dispatcher is aided by a computer storage of regular riders
which is printed out daily. A two-way radio is used to contact the
drivers. The system began in September 1971 with one-way fares set
at 30¢. Ridership has now leveled off. Since the fares cover only
70% of the operating costs, the system is subsidized by the local city
government. The system was designed as a feeder system and plans are
being made to expand it as such. It is interesting to note that high-
income areas provide the greatest proportion of riders.

Dial-a-Ride in Columbus, Ohio covers 2½ square miles, using five
Flexette buses; 450 passengers are carried daily who must pay 25¢ for
a one-way trip. The system operates from 5:00 a.m. until 10:00 p.m.
weekdays, and from 8:00 a.m. to 8:00 p.m. on Saturdays and Sundays.
The driver is contacted via two-way radio. There are 21 checkpoints
in the area from which the driver can call in to the dispatcher.

Six minibuses, each seating nineteen riders, service La Habre,
California's 6½ square miles. The system started in February 1973
and has increased each month to the present 9,000 passengers. The 50¢
fare covers 20% of the operating costs and the county picks up the
rest of the tab. It is reported that most of the users of the Dial-
a-Ride are traditional transit riders who do not own cars.

A summary of the above information on the nine systems surveyed
is shown in Table 1.

3. An Evaluation of Experiences with Demand Responsive Transit

Based on the experience to date, a successful demand responsive system can be operated on a small scale. In this context, success means that the decision makers involved consider the service valuable enough to continue it.

A more objective measure of success is hard to come by. It appears unlikely that a high percentage of demand responsive transit systems can be self-sustaining from fare revenue. The systems that come closest to being self-sustaining are blessed with the ability to charge relatively high fares without discouraging usage and have extraordinary low labor costs. It should be noted that the difference between using full-time professional drivers and using part time drivers at typical pay scales for part time work can often amount to a factor of two.

However, a measure of efficiency which can be used to evaluate demand responsive transit services is the relationship of the cost of providing such service to the cost of alternative services. For example, if the costs of demand responsive transit service are greater than the cost of taxicab service for the same travel demand, then, a transit service is not justified.

From a larger point of view, there are many cases where demand responsive transit service is justified. It can be used to reduce parking requirements in areas where land for parking is at a premium; for example, suburban railroad stations. In certain situations the availability of demand responsive transit service can reduce the cost of providing specialized transportation for the handicapped. Finally, and perhaps most importantly, demand responsive systems are capable of providing increased mobility for the general population in areas where there is a significant demand for improved mobility and where conventional transit would be unable to provide an adequate level of service.

The desire to make use of newly available technology, such as computers and advanced communications equipment, has been behind some of the work on demand responsive transit systems. However, many systems utilize a minimum amount of sophisticated technology.

The use of such technology should be treated as a means to an end, not as an end in itself. A small demand responsive system, using one person in the dispatching office, will gain little from the use of advanced technology.

As the system expands, the introduction of advanced technology should be viewed as a means of minimizing the requirement for additional dispatching personnel. The tradeoff between personnel and hardware should be examined carefully and the temptation to utilize advanced technology should be tempered by an assessment of its real value in providing a higher quality or a lower cost service. Some comments on computer usage are presented later.

A wide variety of vehicles have been used for demand responsive service. These range from modified small vans, such as the Ford Econoline, to Twin Coaches. In between these two extremes in size, several manufacturers produce small buses that have been used for demand responsive services. These vehicles are generally marketed by a body manufacturer and utilize a delivery truck or motor home chassis manufactured by one of the big three automobile firms.

Experience to date had indicated that there is no really satisfactory vehicle for demand responsive transit services. Generally, the modified small vans and the small integral transit buses have been proven to have lower operating costs and greater reliability than the body-on-chassis type buses. However, for the majority of applications, a 10-seat van is too small and the transit bus with a minimum of 25 seats is too large. In at least one case, the space available in a small transit bus has been utilized for deluxe seating.

In conclusion, the successful operation of a demand responsive transit system depends upon careful design and management of the system. There is no standard type that can be used. Each community desiring this type of service will have to evaluate the real potential of the service and the cost of providing it on an individual basis.

However, a considerable body of experience is available to draw upon in such areas as usage estimation, dispatching system designs, vehicle selection, and management organization.

D.   SYSTEMS APPROACH TO MAINTENANCE AND SCHEDULING

In their desire to meet increasing demands for an efficient public transportation system at low cost, transportation authorities are
beginning to turn to new technological methods which can increase the
effective use of their resources. Two areas which readily lend themselves to these new methods are fleet management and bus scheduling.

A fleet management system gives the administrator a completely
modern tool to control his vehicle costs in all areas, from purchasing to final disposition, including all phases of maintenance. Public Technology, Inc. and the American Public Works Association are
jointly developing such a computer-based system which will be applicable to any type of fleet operation. UMTA has funded development of
a similar program directly applicable to bus fleet operations (SIMS),
which will be made available to all transportation authorities shortly.
With such tools, the costly process of maintenance and replacement
can be greatly streamlined and the savings passed on to the public in
the form of improved service.

Improved service is also the objective of the scheduling department which is responsible for the development of efficient timetables
and the allocations of vehicles and drivers. Making schedules is a
time consuming and exacting task requiring the services of imaginative
and experienced people who must spend substantial amounts of time en-
gaged in tedious, repetitive computations.

The development of good geographic data bases which can indicate
where people are, what their income levels are, what their mobility
is, and how those particular factors interface at any particular time
with a particular proposal for a bus route or for the evaluation of
existing bus routes, are important factors to be considered. Furthermore, there is need for the ability to change these data on a day-to-
day basis, or on a year-to-year basis as the public demand shifts.
Sometimes well-calculated guesses are necessary to estimate what the
demand might be. In Europe, notably in Germany, several systems have
been developed which interface transportation alternatives with good
socio-economic data bases to give reliable information for route decision making.

These tasks can now be greatly simplified by the use of modern, computer-based tools. UMTA has funded the development of a package which can assist in headway sheet development, vehicle scheduling, and driver run cutting. Its application would free important and highly skilled manpower resources which can then be brought to bear on more complex and demanding problems.

It is through the use of such advanced technologies that transit authorities can successfully meet the challenge of the urban problem and continue to provide high-quality service.

III. SOLID WASTE COLLECTION TECHNOLOGY

DAVID MARKS

Massachusetts Institute
of Technology
Cambridge, Massachusetts

PROBLEM STATEMENT

Discuss and expose available new technology and new software systems for handling solid waste management effectively.

A. INTRODUCTION

It is most appropriate that a conference on urban technology turn its attention to a major urban system that is vital to the metabolic processes of urban areas. The term waste management system is used to define the system which starts with resource use and the resultant waste generation, through transportation storage, resource recovery attempts and treatments, to final disposal in the environment. Normally, we consider three types of wastes: solid, liquid, and gaseous; it is clear that there are major interactions and transformations between these processes. That is, a major source of air pollution is the burning of solid wastes; liquid wastes represent for the most part solid material diluted in water as a transport medium. This particular overview will center on the management of solid wastes because it represents a problem which not only is one of great and growing urgency to urban areas but one in which major technology advances are needed or have been defined but not truly implemented.

Like all public systems, the technology of the problem cannot be considered in a vacuum as a purely technical exercise. The management of solid wastes has major economic, social, and political impacts which must be defined and evaluated as well in order to bring about the implementation of a successful plan. The entire field is littered with case studies of new technology which could not be instituted because no institution was available to spread the costs among the users, because disequities of a treatment facility built to serve an area such as noise, traffic, and decreased land values mostly fall on one small segment of the community, or because new procedures may involve changing basic societal habits, perceptions, or involvement. This overview will attempt to deal with the technology questions and the issue of successful implementation within a complex urban setting.

B. THE SOLID WASTE MANAGEMENT SYSTEM

The solid waste management system can be thought of as a series of processes which start with resource use and end with final disposal of the end products of that use in the environment. Its important elements are shown in Figure 1.

As indicated, we consider several major tasks as making up the solid waste management system: (1) resource use; (2) waste generation; (3) on-site processing, treatment, and storage; (4) collection and transportation; (5) storage and processing; (6) treatment; (7) resource recovery; and (8) final disposal in the environment.

Let us examine this system as it deals with a typical urban process; that is, the solid waste generated in urban areas for which municipalities assure responsibility. Such systems move about 125 million tons of material per year in the United States at a total cost of about $4 billion. While most technology applications in the past

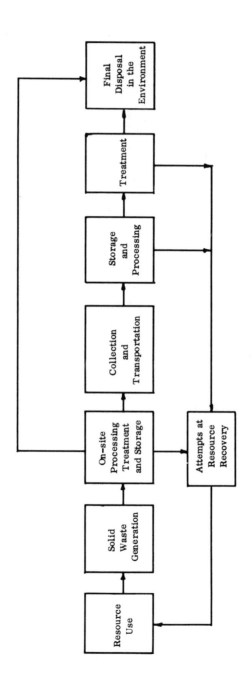

FIG. 1. The Solid Waste Management System

have been devoted to the technology of disposal, in fact, 80% of the cost shown is in collection, and most of these costs are labor costs involved in the physical handling and transferring of materials in the collection process. With waste loads increasing at 5% per year, labor costs rising and many resources becoming scarcer and more expensive, the system demands more detailed attention and management. Let us consider the elements involved and the options available in such a system.

1. Resource Use and Waste Generation

The United States is a highly affluent society having only a small portion of the world's population (less than 10%) yet using a large proportion of its resources, about 40%. This is clearly evident in the resource use picture in the average municipality. On the order of 4 to 5 pounds a day of waste material are produced per person. The composition of that waste (about 40% paper, 10% glass, 10% ferrous and nonferrous metals, 25% plastics, textiles, rubber, and miscellaneous, and only 15% food and organic material) indicates two major points.

First, much of the waste material, being non-organic, could in fact be kept out of the waste stream. This would require consideration of the true social costs, along with the ordinary economic costs, upon which consumers decide what will be wasted and what won't. The amount and composition of municipal waste is both a measure of our affluence and our inability to include social costs in private economic decisions.

Second, the diverse nature and composition of the waste products makes it not a very "rich" ore for later processing and resource recovery. Later, we will see a great deal of technological interest in separating this waste back into its individual components for recovery purposes. Obviously, non-technological attempts, such as economic incentives or legal processes or technological processes which are less resource intensive, that would change the character of the waste produced are an important area of investigation. However, little detailed study has been made in this area.

2. On-Site Processing, Storage, and Treatment

In this area many technological and non-technological advances have been made. Processing is directed toward technology that reduces bulk such as in-home compactors and industrial shredders, or changes its form like garbage grinders, so it can be introduced into the liquid waste system. Some municipal systems require presorting of wastes and provide separate collection. But this is often hard to enforce or motivate and is costly. Storage problems have been partially solved through the developments in new container technology such as plastic bags and dumpster containers. On-site treatment has been centered on incineration, but such technology is under considerable attack because of its inefficiency and resultant air polluting emissions. This is an obvious area for new technological applications.

3. Collection and Transportation

As noted, collection and transport are the most expensive elements of the system and are usually operated, or at least controled, by municipal government. Because of the strong externalities to society in urban settings of uncollected wastes, the public sector has found it easier to collect waste as a public function and thus avoid community problems caused by individual lack of cooperation. Most collection is carried out by labor crews who pick up containers and empty them into collection vehicles. Since this operation is the single largest expense in the system, it has received considerable interest from researchers.

Much of the difficulty in analyzing this function stems from its nonuniformity. Some collection workers are public employees; others are not. Some systems collect at the curb, others from back yards. Collection frequency varies from once a week to once a day. Vehicles range from small trucks to 35 cubic yard monsters, with a variety of sizes in between. Collection crews vary in size from a single driver-collector to a crew of five.

Operations research and computer science have been applied to the development of efficient routing, work schedules, equal assignments, and productivity analysis and have been used to perform other analytical functions aimed at increasing efficiency. New technology in vehicles includes more automated trucks with mechanical arms to scoop up containers, and scooter trains that collect small trash carts and bring them to larger collection vehicles. Since collection vehicles are not efficient long-haul transporters, transfer stations have been build for consolidation and sorting of materials for reshipment by railroad or large tractor trailers. This will be discussed further in Large-Scale Storage and Processing.

An important technological advance has been the recent introduction of vacuum pipelines for waste transportation. Many installations have been made in Europe and are being made now in the United States for housing developments, hospitals, and commercial establishments. The most noteworthy large-scale application has been done by Envirogenics, Inc. under Swedish license for the new Walt Disney World in Florida. The attraction of such a system is its elimination of large labor forces and the ability to operate efficiently in all types of weather.

The most important problems to be faced in a collection system are the technology for better collection (either in pipes or vehicles) and non-technical studies of managing public work forces, including the scheduling of work and establishment of productivity measures.

4. Large-Scale Storage and Processing

The use of large commercial or municipal facilities for storing, transferring, or processing waste before it is disposed of is becoming more and more prominent. A transfer station can be used not only as a place where loads are assembled for more suitable transport, but as a place where the processing and sorting for final disposal and resource recovery can also be accomplished. Several United States cities have adopted this concept and find it quite efficient. Of course, with these facilities, as well as any other large-scale public facility, effciency and cost justification must also be weighed against the social disbenefits of a noisy, busy, and potentially offensive facility. Citizens are very happy to gain the efficiency provided the facility isn't in their neighborhood. If it is to be located nearby, they will vigorously and vocally oppose such construction.

5. Resource Recovery

Resource recovery deals with the attempts to process waste as an "urban ore", that is, to extract its important components for reuse. It seems very odd to take a waste so rich in resources and potential energy and simply get rid of it. There have been successful attempts at garnering energy from the burning of waste for steam and electricity production on a limited basis. Also, from time to time over the last century, the economic value of some components such as junk cars, waste paper, used tires, and tin cans has been profitable enough to attract the private sector into participation in separate collection. For the most part, however, once wastes are mixed and enter the collection process the problem of separating the various components has proved to be a major technological and economic stumbling block. Thus we pay money to dispose of waste, rather than attempt to gain usable valuable material from it.

Generally, two types of resource recovery systems are considered: those that attempt to separate metals, paper, and glass from the rest and those that attempt to deal with the remaining wastes after the separation step. Processes such as size reduction, screening, vibrating sorters, electronic scanners, magnets, shredders, air classifiers, and a variety of other schemes have all been applied, but no satisfactory system has yet been developed to produce the truly homogeneous separation necessary for inexpensive, competitive input to new resource use.

Energy conversion of the remaining products has also not seen considerable development, although technology has been suggested for the generation of methane gas from organics, conversion to other fuels including fuel for gas turbine generation of electricity and burning for heat value, and composting for fertilizer. While much technological investigation has taken place in this area, even more is needed.

6. Treatment

By treatment we mean those processes designed to reduce materials to innocuous forms without, or after, an attempt at resource recovery.

The most familiar technology is the incinerator (burning at high temperatures in the presence of oxygen) of which there are many hundreds in the United States, the largest of which is a 1600 ton per day unit in Chicago. These capital-intensive facilities ($6,000 to $20,000 per ton per day for construction; $7 to $10 per ton for operation) are helpful in that they reduce waste volume and offensiveness yet require little land area. However, they are a major air pollution source and the present technology necessary to meet air quality standards is very expensive and not terribly reliable. In addition, the solid residue (about 3%) must still be disposed of. As noted earlier, it is difficult to locate new incineration facilities because of neighborhood pressures.

Another new technology which is only now being developed on the municipal scale is pyrolysis which is the breaking down of complex compounds using heat in the absence of oxygen. This represents a technology transfer from coal liquification techniques and thus has considerable justification even though it has not yet been fully tested at real scale on solid waste. Waste reduction is expected to be 90%, with no air pollution, but with a liquid waste problem. Costs, while not yet fully refined, seem in the order of magnitude of incineration.

7. Disposal

The cheapest method of final disposal, both for untreated wastes and for the residual from treatment processes is systematic burial in the ground in a sanitary land fill. This method is quite land-intensive and requires that waste be covered each day to cut down on vermin, burning, and litter. It should not be confused with past practices of open dumping which is currently the major means of final disposition. In this method, little attempt is made to minimize air pollution or vermin. Moreover, water pollution problems can occur if no attention is paid to correct procedures.

8. Overview of the System

From the discussion of the system, several important areas suggest themselves for technology application and development. First, in
terms of resource use and waste generation, new technology for pack-
aging and processes which are less resource-intensive are necessary.
The designer can no longer ask only what is coming out of the end of
the pipe in order to design, but must also ask himself what goes into
the pipe in the first place. This requires non-technological studies
of ways to change resource use patterns and preferences for certain
types of resource use. New technology for at-the-site processing of
wastes such as low air polluting incinerators, separators, and compactors are also needed. For collection, new technology in vehicle
and pipeline methods, as well as studies of efficient management of
work forces, are required.

Resource recovery has many important technology needs for separation of wastes for use and reuse in energy production. New technology is also needed for pyrolysis, incineration, and the attendant
air pollution problems. The most vital problem in sound environmental disposal is the impact of waste emissions on air, land, and water.
Substantive research must be done to further refine quality standards
and to balance them against other developmental factors. The close
interrelationship between the various types of wastes can mean that
close concentration on one type may bring improvement at the expense
of another. This must be an important consideration when solid waste
management systems are devised.

Further, a system is not necessarily optimized by optimizing its
individual components. The system must be considered on the whole.
This means that one should look for those parts of the system where
changes can bring about the best responses to the objectives of the
entire system.

It is also important to realize that economic cost minimization
is not the only objective for a system. In fact, it is because many
factors do not have internalized economic costs associated with them
that solid waste management is a problem at all.

Consideration of how the disutilities of the system fall upon different individuals is also extremely important. From an efficiency point of view, regional cooperation and transport of waste by rail to rural areas even 200 miles away is a very realistic alternative. However, politically and socially, every attempt to do this has failed because of the reluctance of the rural areas to accept the waste despite financial incentives. This is a common public sector problem needing not only research, but recognition by practitioners as well. A good technical solution cannot be implemented unless the questions about who will pay for it and who will be hurt by it are successfully addressed in a public forum. That fact may be difficult for technologists to accept, but this is the nature of the public sector. The urban technology game is not only technology for its own ends, but for the service of society in its many different forms and interest groups. To learn this is the most important step towards successful technology transfer in this area.

PANEL SUMMARY

In this session, a variety of issues were addressed, both of a hard and a soft technology nature. The wide-ranging problems associated with solid waste management were kept in view. Valuable data, options, and methods were presented which offered the attendees new concepts and ideas with which to return to their home base.

Let us first consider technology and equipment oriented problem areas. In terms of recycling, many of the comments, as reported in the volume on UTC 2, were heard. At present, we are recycling roughly 2% to 3% of our refuse. Markets and actual prices for reclaimed materials must be firmly established so that equipment and sorter manufacturers can begin to appreciate requirements and eventual payoff. A complex "automatic man-picking" system, developed at Massachusetts Institute of Technology and presently in the testing and modeling stage, was disclosed. Using advanced sensors, coupled to a computer, a wide variety of materials can be identified and separated. Clearly, success on at least a reasonable scale is needed before nationwide implementation can even be considered.

The important work on mechanized refuse collection being done in Scottsdale, Arizona afforded the participants an opportunity to see a variety of new and useful equipment. These included nonstop can and bag collection devices, and large-scale, single-man automated front loaders for large refuse containers. Typical costs of operation for these drop into the range of private industry, i.e., $1.50 per hour per month; these devices can load 30 to 40 tons per man-day (or per crew shift since only one operation is required). With such efficiency, it is clear that treatment of solid waste becomes the overriding problem, rather than its collection. Transferability of vehicles developed in the relatively flat, inclement-weather-free Southwest to other terrains and climates remains to be seen. Certainly, experiments in other locations are required to assure widespread utility.

The nature of funding these developments was raised. Since most of this new technology was, in fact, generated by government (Environmental Protection Agency) grants, there are many questions for the private sector equipment manufacturer. Indeed, when do they become involved in the research, design, development, and marketing aspects? How can municipal governments encourage this to happen? Conceivably, institutions like Public Technology, Inc. can assist, but more seem necessary.

As part of this panel review we cover here the routing and scheduling by computer of sanitation services as presented at the conference. Many algorithms presently exist and more are being developed to minimize collection costs. Basic parameters include distance, time, vehicle maintenance, and crew cost.

Methods for addressing these problems include variations of some classical routing procedures: minimizing travel by assuring only one visit per site (house, multiple dwelling, etc.), minimizing travel by decreasing the number of traverses per street, and workload equilization. In the discussion of these techniques it was stressed that important interaction between developers and users (the sanitation unions) was vital. There is a distinct place and need for human intercession and judgment in the generation of optimal scheduling, etc., and therefore it should be encouraged.

Now let us turn out attention to the policy issues which arose. Of prime importance in this regard was the extensive New York City experience over the last three years and the dramatic improvements in productivity attained. In 1969, the sanitation service was the most complained about in the city; by 1973 it was held up as a model! The general techniques used there appear to be eminently transferrable, in particular, to other cities' sanitation systems, and in general, to many civil service agencies. Note that the gains cited below did not result from increases in the size of the trucks (New York uses a 20-yard vehicle which is constrained by street dimensions), nor increases in the three-man crew size, nor increases in containerization (only 5% of the total refuse collected). Actually, a complete management-by-objective (MBO)[*] system was utilized.

It may be worthwhile at this point to review the steps in the New York experience to understand the issues which had to be addressed to assure proper viability. Initially, new professional management was provided for the sanitation department; these outsiders generally had strong analytical backgrounds. The former top-level individuals had risen through the ranks of civil service bureaucracy and appointments were usually politically motivated.

One of the first jobs for the new management team was an in-depth study of trucks and broom maintenance. Union practices had suggested equipment maintenance at roughly one half the speed of comparable private industry. To see if better standards could be met, a new shop was established and staffed by probationary employees (those not subject to the union contract). Private industrial standards were met. After considerable discussion with the union (and some relaxation of performance by about 10%), New York City now meets 45 basic maintenance standards set by the private sector.

Management control and productivity were the next major problems to be studied. The role of the union was an important one here; however, the city made it clear to the employees that items like produc-

---

[*] It will be recognized that this is an application of MBO to city government, as described in Reference 1.

tivity were strictly management prerogatives and would be addressed without union consent, if need be. Like the classic MBO mold, goals were determined with labor and management side-by-side on a month-to-month basis. Each field unit was considered separately and 23 programmatic measures were set up for monitoring.

The effectiveness of the overall program can be seen from the following data for 1970, before the program was instituted, and for 1973, after three years of operation.

	In 1970	In 1973
Maintenance		
Collection trucks out of service	38%	10%
Mechanical brooms out of service	45%	20%
Services		
Collection amounts	8 tons per crew shift	10 tons per crew shift
Collections missed	20%	less than 1%
Collections at night	27%	less than 1%
Streets missed by mechanical broom	19%	less than 1%

The improvements attained in this program are very impressive. However, as stressed over and over again, and it cannot be overemphasized, it is most essential that strong union involvement be a major factor in any new management process from its inception. To impose demands later just doesn't work. Management (in this instance, city government) must be straight with its employees, discuss the methodology, review the needs and objectives of the program and give the unions a strong role in development.

This panel session was one of the most fruitful of the conference. In summarizing it, we find that many of the ideas voiced at UTC 2 were heard again, but now in different casts as on-going progress was reported.

REFERENCE

1. Fox, H., "Urban Technology: A Primer on Problems," Marcel Dekker, Inc., New York, 1973.

BIBLIOGRAPHY

Abert, J. G. and Fusman, M. J., "Resource Recovery: A New Field for Technology Application," <u>American Institute of Chemical Engineers Journal</u>, 18 (6), November 1972.

Appell, H. R., Wender, I., and Muller, R., "Conversion of Urban Refuse to Oil," Bureau of Mines, Solid Waste Program, Technical Report, 1970.

Bjeerkman, A. A., "Swedish Underground Pipeline Vacuum Network Serves 3,000 Apartments," <u>Refuse Removal Journal</u>, 10(3), March 1969.

Clark, R. M. and Toffner, R. O., "Financing Municipal Solid Waste Management Systems," <u>Journal of the Sanitary Engineering Division</u>, American Society of Civil Engineering, 96 (SA4), August 1970.

DeGeare, T. V., Jr. and Ongerth, J. E., "Empirical Analysis of Commercial Solid Waste Generation, "<u>Journal of the Sanitary Engineers</u> Division, American Society of Civil Engineers, 97 (SA6), December 1971.

Dornby, N. L., Hull, H. E. and Testin, R. F., "Recovery and Utilization of Municipal Solid Waste, Environmental Protection Agency, SW-10c, 1971.

Engdahl, R. B., "Solid Waste Processing: A State of the Art Report on Unit Operations and Processes, "Environmental Protection Agency, PHS Publication 1856, Washington, D.C., 1969.

Golucke, C. G. and McGauley, G. H., "Comprehensive Studies of Solid Waste Management," Vols. I, II, III. 1970-71, Environmental Protection Agency, Office of Solid Waste Management, Washington, D.C.

Hickman, H. L., "Characteristics of Municipal Solid Wastes,"<u>Scrap Age</u>, 26 (2), February 1969.

Kown, B. and Kass, E. A., "Put Refuse in a Pipe, Let Air Do the Work," <u>The American City</u>, June 1973.

Marks, D. H., Hudson, J., and Fuertes, L., "Analysis Models for Solid Waste Collection," MIT Department of Civil Engineering, Report 72-37 prepared for the Environmental Protection Agency.

Mullen, G. M., "Preliminary Economic Analysis of the GR&D Pyrolysis Process for Municipal Solid Wastes," Garrett Research Development Corp., 1971.

National Center for Resource Recovery, Washington, D.C. Considerable material available on all aspects of resource recovery systems.

Niessen, W. R. and Chansky, S. H., "The Nature of Refuse," Proceedings of 1970 National Incinerator Conference, Cincinnati, Ohio, May 17-20, 1970, published by American Society of Mechanical Engineers, New York, 1970.

Quan, J. E., Tanaka, M., and Charnes, A., "Refuse Quantities and Frequency of Service," Journal of the Sanitary Engineering Division,
American Society of Civil Engineers, 94 (SA2), April 1968.

Rogers, C. A., "Refuse Collection and Refuse Characteristics," Public Works, 97 (3), March 1966.

Straiger, M. G., "We Automated Residential Refuse Collection," American City, 85 (11), November 1970.

Sullivan, P. M. and Stanczy, M. H., "Economics of Recycling Metal and
Minerals from Urban Refuse," Technical Progress Report, Bureau of
Mines, Solid Waste Research Program, April 1971.

Truitt, M. and Liebman, J. C., "Mathematical Modeling of Solid Waste
Collection Policies," Environmental Protection Agency, PHS 2030,
Washington, D.C.

Wilson, D. G., "The Treatment and Management of Urban Solid Waste,"
Technonic Publishing Company, Westport, Connecticut, 1972

IV. AIR AND WATER POLLUTION ABATEMENT
UTILIZING EARTH OBSERVATION SATELLITES[*]

LAWRENCE R. GREENWOOD

NASA Langley Research Center
Hampton, Virginia

PROBLEM STATEMENT

A cost-effective method is needed to assess the state
of the environment in urban areas and to evaluate the
future impact of candidate strategies for enhancing
air and water quality. The use of remote sensing from
aircraft and earth observation satellites is discussed.

----

[*] Because of the relative newness of remote sensing as applied to
urban problems, this panel session was devoted to a tutorial-type discussion. Its major purpose was to present the beginnings of these
techniques to local governments so that they might appreciate the
impacts of Earth Resource Technology Satellites (ERTS) data on their
pollution abatement and land use planning activities. The problem
statement is thus written as an expository view of such techniques
rather than in the form presented elsewhere in this report.

1. Air Pollution

Currently the most serious pollutants are known to be sulfur oxides, particulate matter, carbon monoxide, hydrocarbons, photochemical oxidants, and nitrogen oxides. Pollutants enter the atmosphere as a result of energy conversions (e.g., electrical power generation, burning, vehicle operation) and materials processing and are directly associated with increased demands of the nation for energy and goods. Naturally occurring chemical and physical processes contribute to the aggregate amounts of those pollutants already existing in the atmosphere, e.g., pollen and dust storms. The natural atmosphere serves as a sink for both man-made and naturally occurring pollutants. Nature's limitation as a sink is not known, but we must become concerned when amounts of man-made pollutants begin to approach large fractions of natural levels.

Table 1 gives the estimated emissions of air pollutants for 1970 as reported by the United States Environmental Protection Agency (EPA) (1). These data ignore the geographical distribution of pollutant emission and do not show the effects of the pollutants

TABLE 1

Estimated Emissions of Air Pollutants
by Weight (Millions of Tons)
Nationwide 1970 (Preliminary Data)

	Carbon monoxide	Particulates	Sulfur dioxide	Hydrocarbon	Nitrogen oxides
Transportation	111.0	0.7	1.0	19.5	11.7
Fuel combustion in stationary sources	0.8	6.8	26.5	0.6	10.0
Industrial processes	11.4	13.1	6.0	5.5	0.2
Solid waste disposal	7.2	1.4	0.1	2.0	0.4
Miscellaneous	16.8	3.4	0.3	7.1	0.4
Total	147.2	25.4	33.9	34.7	22.7
Percentage change 1969-1970	-4.5	-7.4	0	0	+4.5

Source: EPA

Figure 1 pictures the long-term trends for the ambient air levels of three major pollutants: CO, SO_2, and total suspended particles (TSP). These data are presented as pollutant concentrations which, like the pollution weight estimates, do not indicate the comparative damage different pollutants can cause. Despite some indications of downward trends, large regions of the nation exceed the primary air quality standards and even with stricter controls, it is estimated that the urban industrial regions will still not meet the standards in 1975 (3).

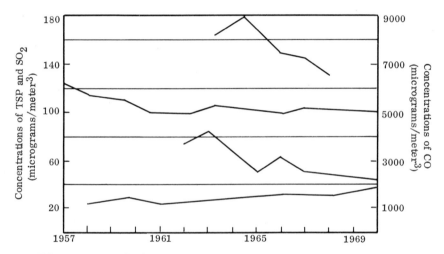

FIG. 1. Trends in ambient levels of selected air pollutants. From top to bottom, the 4 individual graph lines represent (1) Urban CO in 6 U.S. cities, (2) urban TSP in 60 U.S. cities, (3) urban SO_2 in 21 U.S. cities, and (4) nonurban-originating TSP in 20 U.S. cities. TSP = total suspended particulates. (From Ref. 2.)

EPA has estimated the direct monetary costs associated with air pollution damages to human health, materials and vegetation, and to property values. These costs exceed $16 billion per year, distributed as shown in Table 2.

TABLE 2

Annual Economic Losses Due to Air Pollution

Impacted areas	Billions of dollars	Percentage
Vegetation/materials	4.9	31
Property values	5.2	32
Human health	6.0	37

2. Water Pollution

Since water plays a vital role in terrestrial lifeforms, pollution of any significant part of the earth's water supply, whether it be salt water or fresh, is a serious concern. Although water often contains most of the chemical elements and a large number of compounds, water pollutants can generally be classified under several broad categories. Table 3 categorizes the major types of water pollution and some of the sources, together with the uses most affected.

Most water pollution can be characterized as a problem that is aggravated by growing population and expanding industrial demands. The concentration of population centers at specific points on lakes and rivers and in the coastal zones makes water pollution more of a local or regional problem than a global one. However, there is ample evidence that the world's oceans are also becoming polluted (for instance, DDT pollution is international).

As the Council on Environmental Quality (CEQ) reports, water pollution is most acute in densely settled or industrial sections of the country, and the projections of continued growth of these areas will intensify the water pollution in the continental United States.[2] As specific examples: the waters of the Maumee River in Ohio contain coliform bacteria (an indicator of raw sewage pollution) as high as 24,000 times the maximum allowed by federal drinking standards; carbolic acid is dumped up to 137 times the allowable maximum, and 14

TABLE 3

Major Types and Sources of Water Pollution and the Water Uses Most Affected

Types of pollution	Sources	Water most affected			
		Recreation	Aquatic life	Municipal water supply	Industrial use
Solid waste (bacteria)	Inadequately treated sewage	X		X	X
Sediments	Erosion aggravated by industry and agriculture	X	X	X	X
Organic materials (oil, pesticides, herbicides, phenols, etc.)	Oil from ships, industrial processes, agricultural spraying and runoff	X	X	X	
Inorganic materials (mercury, copper, lead, etc.)	Mining and industrial processes	X	X	X	
Radioactivity	Mining; ore processing; power plants; industrial, medical and other research	X	X	X	X
Heat	Power plants and industrial cooling water	X	X		X
Nutrients (and lack of dissolved oxygen)	Household detergents, agricultural fertilizers, and industrial processes	X	X	X	X

kilograms of cyanide are put into this river per day (4). Millions
of kilograms of phosphate are allowed to enter Lake Erie. This sub-
stance, along with others such as nitrogen, is a nutrient source for
algae growth. Roughly one kilogram of phosphate will support 700 kilograms of algae (Nelson, G., 1967). Consequently, Lake Erie is pro-
ducing vast algae blooms that in turn become polluting factors as the
plants die. The water of southern Lake Michigan is so polluted that
it is estimated that it would take 100 years to clear itself, while
some authorities feel that the damage is irreversible (Nelson, G.,
1967).

It must be emphasized that the offshore waters contiguous to the
United States are also a responsibility. These waters include the
territorial sea and the contiguous zone which covers most of the Continental Shelf regions. This expansive marine environment is being
and will be stressed by man's activities. Stresses come from those
pollutants which find their way to these waters from the winds and
rainfall, from the flow of rivers and estuaries, and from intentional
and accidental dumping of sewage, oil, and other wastes. The losses
of ocean and coastal fisheries and shellfish production caused by the
pollution of the estuaries are substantial. Over one-fifth of the nation's shellfish beds have been closed because of pollution. Despite
the current cost that industries and water users pay for treating polluted water for reuse, CEQ studies have suggested that water pollution
may cause yearly recreational losses extending into many billions of
dollars. Man's future plans for the utilization of the Continental
Shelf regions (for offshore ports, nuclear power plant siting, and
natural resources) will undoubtedly result in additional stress.

3. General

Both the CEQ and the Environment Study Group (1970 Summer Study
Report to the National Academy of Sciences) view the understanding of
the basic ecological and physical processes which determine the fate
and importance of pollutants as the essential goal to an effective
long-range strategy for pollution control. In the opinion of these
and many other groups, improved observational data leading to adequate

prediction and forecasting are necessary to establish pollution standards and evaluate the effectiveness of on-going pollution abatement programs.

Clearly, the development of such a capability will contribute to providing a basis for rational, objective decision making which will help to reduce the emotionally charged, often uninformed power struggle between polluters, government, and environmentalists which now pervades the search for a healthy environment.

B.   CONSTRAINTS OR SPECIFICATIONS

Several factors have been identified which must be resolved in order for remote sensing techniques to be meaningfully applied to the environmental problems confronting our urban areas. These factors are considered below.

1.   The first of these obstacles is the gap between the technologist and the user. Closing this gap and realizing the potential of remote sensing will require highly trained technical staffs of the level of scientific sophistication not readily available at local and state levels.

2.   Secondly, a source for a continuing supply of operational data is needed. While a number of research activities utilizing remotely sensed data have been undertaken, no operational system is presently available to local governments and, therefore, local and state officials must question the investment to train personnel without the assurance of a continuing source of data.

3.   A third factor to be considered in applying remote sensing techniques to an urban area is cost. State and local authorities have a legal requirement to develop and implement a plan that will insure that air and water quality meet federal standards. The plan must be implemented within relatively modest budgets and, therefore, any use of remote sensing must be shown to be cost effective.

4.   Finally, legal questions surrounding the acquisition and use of remotely sensed measurements of air and water quality must be considered. Many legal requirements surrounding the introduction into legal action of remotely sensed data have not been resolved and will certainly have an impact on the role of remote sensing in an overall monitoring system.

C. STATE OF TECHNOLOGY

1. Remote Monitoring

In recent years a number of individuals and organizations have recognized that monitoring is a key element in environmental control. The previous chairman of the CEQ has said, "Our knowledge about the state of the environment and its trends is still primitive in many areas; it will remain so unless and until we develop appropriate monitoring systems...and the means by which the data can be effectively used to manage the environment in a positive way." He indicates that baseline data must be accumulated and that provisions must be made for repeated and continuing observations. Such information is vital in determining environmental needs, priorities, and the effectiveness of control strategies.

The use of remote sensing to monitor air and water quality has been developed in recent years. Several specific contributions which remote sensing can make were summarized by Lawrence and Keafer (5) and are given below.

1. Remote sensing from aircraft or spacecraft affords wide geographic coverage, and therefore, environmental monitoring on a regional and global basis can be performed. While current remote sensing techniques are generally not as accurate as conventional methods of measurement, wide areal coverage by a single instrument of known precision will permit investigations of a number of problems, including dispersal rates and long-term buildup of pollution, tracing the movement of contaminated air and water masses for forecasting pollution levels, and the interaction of pollution levels and meteorology. In addition, remote sensors can assist in determining the proper location for in situ sensors and insure the statistical validity of synoptic measurements by a network of conventional sensors.

2. Remote sensing techniques from ground-based mobile platforms in some cases can make a valuable contribution to the monitoring problem. Violations of emission standards can be discovered with quick look remote measurements and the results validated by conventional techniques for enforcement if legal action is required.

3. The measurement and long-term monitoring of many of the cli-
    matic parameters, including changes in the global heat bud-
    get, appears to be feasible with the use of space-based re-
    mote sensing techniques. In addition, remote sensing has a
    valuable contribution to make in the verification of numeri-
    cal models.

4. The remote interrogation of in situ sensors is an applica-
    tions area with very significant potential. Near-real-time
    data can be obtained from inaccessible areas with substan-
    tial cost savings by using data relay links between conven-
    tional sensors and a data collection center.

Remote sensing techniques, on the other hand, have certain limitations. Remote sensors, based on aircraft and satellite platforms,
generally are designed to measure the total air pollutant vertical
burden in the troposphere, the upper-atmosphere horizontal burden,
secondary effects of water pollution, thermal surface anomalies, and
land-use characterization. The problems of quantitatively measuring
water pollutants at a particular point and the vertical profiles of
air pollutants in the troposphere are not now amenable to solution
by remote sensors based on aircraft and satellite platforms. For a
comprehensive study of application of satellite- and aircraft-based
remote sensors to pollution measurement, reference is made to the report of the Working Group on the Remote Measurement of Pollution (6)
and to NASA Contractor Report CR-1380 (7).

In July 1972, the Earth Resources Technology Satellite, ERTS-1,
was launched. The ERTS program was the first dedicated to demonstrat-
ing the practical applications of space data to monitoring and managing earth resources. The ERTS system is a facility available to all
qualified users. More than 700 proposed studies have been considered
and 334 have been initiated. Of these 334 studies, 83 investigations
are concerned with mineral resources, 62 with agriculture/forestry,
45 with water resources, 40 with land use surveys, 37 with environmental studies, and 29 with marine and ocean surveys. The ERTS system consists of a satellite and ground data handling system that processes the spacecraft sensor data. The sensors aboard ERTS include
a Return Beam Vidicon (RBV) which consists of three high-resolution
television cameras, each fitted with an appropriate spectral filter.

The second imaging sensor aboard ERTS is a Multispectral Scanner System (MSS). It images the surface of the earth in four spectral bands simultaneously. At the altitude of ERTS, an 80-meter-square instantaneous field of view is achieved with the MSS. A third part of the ERTS payload is the Data Collection System (DCS) which relays data gathered by many ground-based data collection platforms deployed in remote locations. These platforms are being used to sample local environmental or surface conditions and can accept as many as eight analog or 64 digital sensors.

On March 5-9, 1973, a symposium of significant results from ERTS was held. A summary (8) was prepared of the results to date of ERTS investigators. The significant results that apply to monitoring air and water pollution will be discussed here.

2. Air Pollution

Results of ERTS-1 investigators have confirmed that with spectral and spatial resolution of the ERTS sensors, one can monitor and assess some specific sources of air pollution. Copeland (8) has used density slicing in the identification of smoke plumes and was able to detect previously unreported emission sources leading to possible

law-enforcement applications. Smoke plumes over Lake Michigan have been studied by Lyons (8) and he connected their occurrence to snow showers. The observation of the condensation trails from high-flying aircraft have been noted by a number of investigators.

3. Water Pollution

Chemical discharge from a paper mill on Lake Champlain has been detected by ERTS. Along with aircraft photographs, the ERTS data are being used in court to obtain a cease and desist order against the polluter.

The use of ERTS imagery to detect sediment in rivers and streams has been studied by several investigators. The turbidity of major reservoirs in Kansas has been studied by Yarger (8), and the results showed good agreement with suspended load measurements

The use of ERTS imagery for detecting ocean dumps of industrial waste was demonstrated by Mairs, Wezernak and Fontane (8). It is possible to use the ERTS imagery to monitor the location of dumping to assure compliance with regulations.

A number of investigators have focused on the near shore environment and have studied rate and extent of beach erosion (Slaughter and Mairs), long-term changes in shoreline configuration (Kerhin), monitoring of wetlands (Anderson, Carter, and McGinness; Klemas and Bartlett; Brown, Meyer, Ulliman, Prestin, Trippler, Gamble and Eller; Clapp, Kiefer, McCarthy and Niemann), and mapping of general plant communities (Anderson). Gilbertson and Jensen have used ERTS imagery to detect algae blooms and red tide encroachment of fresh and saline bodies.

ERTS will only be a first step in utilizing spacecraft to monitor air and water pollution. NASA presently plans a Nimbus G spacecraft in 1977, the thrust of which will be to study in more depth the remote measurement of air and water quality from space. Typical sensors being developed for air pollution measurements (and being considered for Nimbus G are shown in Table 4 (5). In addition, some of the instruments included in Figure 7 (i.e., MAPS, HSI, COPE, and LIDAR) can be flown on aircraft systems or used for ground-based studies of air quality. Similar instruments being developed for water quality investigations are shown in Table 5 (6).

SUMMARY

Air and water pollution in our urban areas are, indeed, super-problems. Although there are some indications that progress is being made, difficulties in meeting future air and water quality standards loom large. It is universally recognized that a more concerted effort is needed for effective solution. Measurements of environmental quality are essential for determining needs, establishing priorities, and for evaluating the effectiveness of control strategies and abatement programs. Remote sensing of air and water quality from aircraft and spacecraft have a potential for making significant contributions

TABLE 4

Typical Air Quality Remote Sensing Instruments

Experiment	Measurement capability	Instrument features	Modeling and data interpretation
LACATE - Lower atmosphere composition and temperature	Vertical profiles of trace gases (O_3, HNO_3, N_2O, H_2O, CH_4, NO_2) Temperature profile in lower stratosphere	IR limb-scanned radiometer Large telescope Cooled detector	Inversion of radiance values to constituent profiles
MAPS - Monitoring air pollution from a satellite	Column densities of trace gases (SO_2, NO_2, NH_3, CH_4, CO_2, CO)	IR radiometer Gas-filter correlation analyzer Colled detector	Inversion of radiance values to constituent profiles
RPM - Visible radiation polarization measurements	Polarization characteristics of scattered sunlight Characteristics of aerosols (by inference)	Photopolarimeter	Modeling and data interpretation is challenging task
HSI - High speed interferometer	Absorption spectra of trace gases	IR interferometer spectrometer High resolution with speed scan	Experiment requires transmission and sophisticated processing of with large amounts of data

TABLE 4 (CONTINUED)

Experiment	Measurement capability	Instrument features	Modeling and data interpretation
COPE - Carbon-monoxide pollution experiment	Column densities of trace gases -- CO, CH_4	Near infrared Correlation interferometer	Inversion of radiance values to constituent burden
MULTI-POLLUTANT - Version of COPE instrument	Column densities of trace gases - CO, CH_4	Infrared Correlation interferometer	Present SRT effort limited to preliminary design study of experiment requirements
Tunable laser heterodyne radiometer	Improve sensor specificity and sensitivity	Visible, infrared Improved front end for spectral radiometers	Present SRT effort limited to experimental feasibility study for SO_2, NO_x
LIDAR - Multiple wave-length laser radar	Aerosols and trace gases	Steerable 48" and 24" for ground-based laser radar	Theoretical and experimental laboratory studies of scattering characteristics of aerosols and trace gases

TABLE 5

Sensor-Application Correspondence
for Remote Sensing of Pollution[a]

	U/V	Color	Color IR	Multispectral	Multichannel scanning radiometer	Correlation radiometer	Fraunhoffer line discriminator	Pulsed laser system	Low light level devices	IR imager-scanner	Microwave radiometer	Radar	Scintillation detector	Polarimeter
Oil	1	2	3	1	1	1	1	1		2	1	1		1
Suspended sediment		1	1	1	1	2		2						2
Chem. & toxic wastes		2	3	2	2	2	3	2						
Solid wastes		1	1	1	1	2		2						2
Thermal effluents					1*					1	1			
Radioactive wastes													1	
Nutrient wastes		1		1	1	1		2						3
Living organisms — Intro. of species		2	2	2					3					
Living organisms — Bacteria									3					
Living organisms — Red tide		1	1	1	1	1		1						
Living organisms — Human & cul. effluents		1	1	1	1				1	1		1		

(Film cameras: Color, Color IR, Multispectral)

Key: 1 - presently available

2 - under development

3 - potential applications

* - with infrared channel

[a]From Ref. 6

to monitoring and thus to the solution of the problem. In order to
realize this potential, however, a major challenge will be to develop
better communications and thus help close the technological gap between the researcher and the user at the state and local levels.

REFERENCES

1. "Environmental Quality," Third Annual Report of the Council on
    Environmental Quality, August 1972.

2. "Environmental Quality," Second Annual Report of the Council on
    Environmental Quality, August 1971.

3. "Implementation Plans Get EPA Approval," Environmental Science
    and Technology, Vol.7, No.7, July 1972, p.599.

4. Nelson, G., "The Natural Pollution Scandal," The Progressive, Feb-
    ruary 1967.

5. Lawrence, James D., Jr. and Keafer, Lloyd S., Jr., "Remote Sensing
    of the Environment," NASA paper presented to the Interagency
    Conference on the Environment, October 17-19, 1972.

6. "Remote Measurement of Pollution," NASA SP-285, 1972.

7. Ludwig, C. B., Bartle, R., and Griggs, M., "Study of Air Pollution
    Detection by Remote Sensors," NASA CR-1380, 1969.

8. Freden, Stanley C., and Mercant, Enrico P., Eds., "Symposium on
    Significant Results Obtained from Earth Resources Technology
    Satellite-1," Vol. III, Discipline Summary Reports,X-650-73-155;
    preprint, NASA Golldard Space Flight Center, May 1973.

V.   EDUCATIONAL TECHNOLOGY

JAMES D. KOERNER

Alfred P. Sloan Foundation
New York, New York

PROBLEM STATEMENT

Inform local government authorities, and others in
terested in urban institutions, of the state of the
art in educational technology and in the use of technology to improve the quality and lower the cost of
formal instruction.

A. BACKGROUND

Those concerned with the application of technology to the solution of urban problems might best approach the field of educational technology with a kind of hopeful skepticism. They should recognize that technology at this point in time offers some interesting though limited possibilities as far as the educational system is concerned. They should recognize that the employment of technology for the solution on a nationwide basis, or even for the alleviation of such problems as poor teaching in schools, or the high cost of education, is still in the future.

Predictions were widely and confidently made in the 1950s to the effect that education by 1970 or 1975, especially primary and secondary education, would be revolutionized by technology, that is, by the new educational technology. Leaders and so-called futurists from the knowledge industry, from government, from education, and from foundations joined in these rosy prognostications. This enthusiasm has now given way to embarrassment and disenchantment as many a corporation has found its Edsel in educational technology. The metaphor is imperfect. The Edsel at least ran; the public just wasn't buying. Educational technology to date cannot be said even to run.

Therefore, the expectations, and indeed in some cases the orders of school boards, state legislatures, and college trustees concerning a collection of gadgets they think of rather vaguely as educational technology are ill advised. One sympathizes with their search for ways to cope with the relentlessly rising costs of education, but to look to technology for rescue at this point in time is like expecting the Brothers Wright to have put their first craft into commercial production and to have carried passengers around the country in it.

Let us be more specific about the reasons for technology's failure to date. First, the equipment itself -- the hardware -- has fallen far short of the claims made for it. Hardly a system even today is equal to its propaganda. The most advanced hardware systems have had serious debugging problems, low reliability, high maintenance, and continue for the most part to be incompatible with other systems inasmuch as manufacturers are not yet able to agree on industry-wide standardization. Moreover, the rate of obsolescence in hardware is so high that capital investments for new or improved systems are a continuous necessity.

Then there is the programming itself -- the software -- which has lagged far behind the hardware, imperfect as the latter has been. One has only to sample the materials that have been prepared for use on either simple or complex teaching devices to realize how rudimentary the state of the art still is. Since educational technology today and tomorrow will be just as good or bad as the quality of stuff available on the machines, one can see a long road ahead before a true technology of education can be developed.

Of course, our ignorance of the education process itself has contributed, as it always does, to the failures. If we knew more about how learning occurs with various kinds of students, if we knew more about intelligence, motivation, the rhythm of learning, the role of repetition, and a great many other things, we could design better machines and better programs to go with them. As it is, our knowledge lends very little precision and a great deal of guesswork to educational technology.

The failures of the past also have something to do with the attitudes of teachers toward the whole notion of technology in education. These attitudes, which need to be taken into account by industrialists and local government officials, seem to get more negative as we go up the educational ladder. Teachers at the elementary school level are more or less open about the possibilities of educational technology (even if teachers' unions are not), those at the secondary level are less open, but still willing to be persuaded, and in many cases are systematic users of technology themselves, and those at the college level look on the whole matter with feelings that range from apathy to hostility. That is the general situation, which leaves room for exceptions.

The dominant attitude among college faculties, where most materials for both pre-college and college level education have been prepared in the past, is not due merely to dislike or distrust. It also
reflects the lack of faculty incentives that has plagued development
efforts in educational technology. Distinguished scholars have not
been willing to invest professional time and energy in a field from
which little recognition can be expected and where royalty rates are
low or nonexistent. Up to now, a professor could expect to make more
money from writing a textbook than a computer program, and he could
gain more professional advancement by scholarly publication than by
tinkering with gadgets aimed at improving instruction.

In addition, faculty members, who now find themselves in the most
severe buyers' market since the Depression, are not aglow with desire
to develop a technology of education which may eliminate jobs. Administrators who find their departments losing enrollment (engineering,
for instance) and who have on their hands a surplus of highly paid,
tenured professors who won't retire for some years, are tempted to
explore the potential of technology or anything else that might reduce the unit costs of education; but it is not easy to persuade the
faculty to take an enthusiastic role, and that is the only kind of
role that would mean anything, in such a threatening exploration.

Even so, the skeptics in both public schools and higher education have had a certain amount of justice on their side, in view of
the overpromotion and underperformance which have characterized the
field of educational technology -- if it is a field -- over the last
25 years. Too often a grand plan to exploit instructional technology
has been drawn up by consultants or other outsiders who have no personal responsibility for carrying it out, a procedure that, as far as
one can judge, has always produced failure. Too often these technol-
ogy-based systems have been thrust upon teachers by administrators
who were enamored of innovation or were simply seeking to cut costs.
Too often the systems have been inconvenient to use; too often they
have imposed an outside star performer on the classroom teacher (on
the theory that technology could put persons who were called master

teachers into every classroom, if not every living room, to the benefit of all); too often the program itself offered no visible advantage
over an ordinary book; too often no decent evaluation was attempted;
and too often support for R & D has been capricious and short term.

Finally, the matter of cost has had its effects. The knowledge
industry proceeded in the 1960s on the incredibly naive assumption
that because education was a gigantic enterprise consuming $60 bil-
lion or $70 billion a year (it consumes more now), it constituted a
mass market for educational technology. To their sorrow, they learned
that upwards of 70% and sometimes more, of a typical school budget was
in salaries, that another 15% or 20% was devoted to fixed costs, and
that very little in any loose money was to be found in the average
budget. They also failed to take into account the fact that professional politics, economic protectionism, and simple inertia are as
alive and well in education as in any other large bureaucratic activity, meaning that big changes of any kind are rarely possible.

So much for the failures. What of the state of the art now, and
how does it relate to the major demands being made today on the edu-
ational system, demands for ever greater access to education, for
greater individualization of instruction, for economy and cost reduction, and for in-service or mid-career training for many kinds of professional people? Does the technology exist with which to help meet
these widespread demands? Or is the situation similar to that faced
by society in its demands for the control of automobile emissions or
for ever greater supplies of energy? We have abundant demands, and
indeed government decrees it, to reduce emissions from the internal
combustion engine to certain levels by 1975; and we have equally abundant demands from all segments of society for more energy, particularly electrical energy. The problem in both cases is that our technology is insufficient to satisfy these demands. No amount of wish-
ing or declamation by environmentalists will create a sufficiency; the
only thing that will create it is more technology.

The state of the art in education is only slightly different.
The technology does exist, in a sense, with which we could at least

begin to meet the demands. It exists, that is, if we think of technology only as hardware, for the physical means for communication between the educator and the student. Let's look at where we are with
the major technological systems.

B. BROADBAND COMMUNICATIONS

We now have the technological ability (one should stress ability
for the systems are not yet installed widely) to deliver a vast number of signals to almost any kind of educational audience at almost
any distance. By means of coaxial cable, microwave, and satellites
(in the future by means of lasers, glass fibers and other exotic devices) we have the capability of creating many kinds of telecommunications networks with more or less unlimited capacity. These networks
could tie educational institutions together as well as tie them to
other kinds of public institutions and directly to homes.

C. COMPUTERS

This technology now offers the educator the means unmatched by
anything else he has ever had available for the lightning processing
of truly vast amounts of whatever information the educator regards as
important in learning. Two major experiments in computer assisted instruction will produce within another two or three years better data
about computer learning than we have had in the past. They are the
PLATO IV project at the University of Illinois which will ultimately
link thousands of time shared terminals to a large central computer,
and a system called TICCIT which is being developed by the MITRE Corporation and which uses a small computer along with a coaxial cable
television system that goes into homes. PLATO and TICCIT are two leading experiments; there are many others. The point is that computer
technology now offers the educator an instrument of great range and
power which he is still far from knowing how to exploit. Too often
today's computer programs continue to demonstrate the truth of the
adage that grew up in the computer trade years ago -- "Garbage in,
garbage out."

D. VIDEO REPRODUCTION

The technology of storing miniature talking pictures on tape or disks or film for later replay at one's convenience, or for immediate reproduction as in the case of live television or Picturephone, is one of the most powerful technologies now available to the educational system. This technology is one of scanning a two-dimensional picture (any kind of picture) and converting it to a series of electrical impulses which at the user's end are then reconverted to the original picture. This same technology, by the way, makes possible facsimile reproduction of newspapers and other printed material over long distances.

Broadband technology can of course be combined with video technology or computer technology to provide a virtually unlimited system for delivering miniature talking pictures or digital data, for sending, in other words, any amount of educational programming with illustrations and sound to any audience. Videotapes do not even require a transmission system, only a transportation system to move them from the originator to the point of playback and from one point of playback to another.

E. MINIATURIZATION

In addition to video technology which is a species of electronic miniaturization, microfiche technology allows a large array of miniature images to be stored on transparent materials for later use at a student's convenience. The material can be re-enlarged on a reading machine or can be reproduced on a piece of paper. Much greater size reduction than afforded by ordinary microfilm is now available. Extreme reductions are possible, as with the 20,000-volume library on American civilization offered by Encyclopedia Britannica, each volume of which comes in the form of a single thin fiche measuring three by five inches. Even greater reductions are possible.

Other technologies may also have potential in education. There are many kinds of audio devices, including one that has all but been forgotten by American educators called radio (the BBC seems to remember, however, as do the radio systems of many other countries). There are multitudinous mechanical gadgets ranging from costly teaching machines to xerographic devices to make instant copies at a cheap price of any kind of document. There is also the ordinary blackboard which is a structural aid made possible by technology. There are even things called books, which are nothing more than visual aids made possible by a technological breakthrough in the middle of the 15th century. And there are still other instruments too numerous to mention that continue to be developed by educational entrepreneurs.

Our original question, then, still needs an answer. Can these assorted technologies do anything to meet the increasing demands for access, individualization, economy, and mid-career training? The answer is very little right now, but possibly a good deal in the future. If we think of the term, educational technology, as meaning more than hardware; if we think of it as an integrated system of teaching and learning for which the cost is reasonable and for which software has been specifically developed, tested in practice, revised, retested, and finally validated, then it is clear that educational technology cannot now meet any of the demands. First, because the major hardware systems have not been built or installed on any scale. For example, there is not a single school system or college or university in the country that is completely wired with a broadband communications system, not to mention a system that can link it to the surrounding community. Second, because the quality of the materials to be delivered on whatever kind of hardware one wants to talk about, ranges from the merely pedestrian to the indefensible.

What is needed to move the state of the art forward is a massive program of R & D, especially on the software side, in the hands of the best teams of scholars, technicians, psychologists, and maybe of experts from entertainment and even advertising, that can be attracted to working in the area of educational technology. With that kind of R & D, educators may in time learn how to ask the right questions of the new communications technologies and conduct the right experiments to test their potential. Educators may finally learn how to use television in a way that exploits rather than wastes its special capacities; they may learn how to take advantage of the immense power of the computer to truly individualize instruction for the first time since Mark Hopkins got off his log; and they may learn how to use to best advantage the miniaturized materials, the audio devices, and other technologies not mentioned above or perhaps not even thought of at this point.

History suggests that new technologies are often overrated in the short run but vindicate their prophets in the long run. This may well be the case with educational technology. How long that term will be no one can say, but it is entirely possible that education, by the turn of the century may look fundamentally different from what it is today, thanks to technology. There is at least a gambler's chance that this will turn out to be true and that the quality of American education will then have caught up with the quantity.

PANEL SUMMARY

In this session there appeared to be basic agreement with the problem statement among the members of the panel and the audience. The chairman and the panel members briefly discussed the state of the art in educational technology and reviewed projects of special promise now in operation. There was general agreement on the principal constraints -- economic, academic, and political that have limited the transfer of technology to the teaching-learning process in the past and that continue to exert a strong influence today.

Recurring throughout the discussion were references to the attitudes of public school teachers and college faculties toward educational technology. Collectively considered, and leaving room for many exceptions, instructional personnel continue to be apathetic or hostile about educational technology, or in some cases merely reluctant and uninformed. Various reasons were cited by the participants to account for these attitudes:

1. Lack of professional or financial incentives in educational technology

2. Fear that technology will eliminate jobs

3. Lack of administrative and professional support, especially in higher education, for persons whose main interest is in teaching, i.e., in pedagogy, an interest that would seem to be a prerequisite for effective work with the technologies of instruction

4. Lack of facilities and technical assistance to make experimental work possible, not to say convenient

5. Lack of persuasive evidence that technology can offer the teacher and the student important advantages over traditional methods, and

6. Lack of funds for sustained, long-term R & D

There was discussion but not consensus about the effect on faculty attitudes of the current retrenchment in educational budgets, the general tightening up of the academic marketplace, and the demands being voiced in many quarters for greater efficiency and productivity in education. Some participants felt that such pressures would create a more open attitude toward technology on the part of the teaching staff, especially if along with the pressures came some positive incentives and other kinds of assistance. Others felt that the attitudes of the present teaching staff would change only slowly, under any conditions, and that emphasis might therefore be given to preparation of the future faculties, persons now enrolled in graduate degree programs who are headed for public school or college teaching. It was stressed that the failure to influence teacher training programs and Ph.D. programs has been characteristic of the new curricula and of educational innovations for many years, a failure that has limited sharply the long-term effectiveness of new methods and materials; and concern was expressed that the same type of failure will continue to be true of educational technology unless deliberate steps are taken to prevent it.

The technology of television was touched on frequently by the panel and in discussion from the floor. Today's high school senior, having been exposed to something like 16,000 hours of network televi-

sion (as against about 11,000 hours of formal schooling) is more visu-
ally oriented than his parents and is accustomed to programming that
is technically professional. When he is exposed to programming that
is technically amateur and, in addition, comes in the form of an un-
inspired lecture that fails to exploit the visual medium, he is not
apt to learn a great deal. To date, television has been used mostly
as a mass lecturing device, and in some instances has been more economical than conventional instruction (although hard data on the economics of instructional television are nonexistent); there was general
agreement by the panel that educators are still far from knowing how
to take advantage of the unique potential of television, a potential
that is demonstrated by such out of school programs as Sesame Street.
Until experimental work on the scale of the Children's Television Workshop is undertaken for older age groups, including the college population, television is likely to remain an underused and misused technological tool in education.

The panel discussed several particular programs and institutions
that seem to have an above average degree of interest and support from
the instructional staff. The New York Institute of Technology (NYIT)
and its extensive experimental work in a wide range of technologies
was discussed. It was notable, however, that NYIT's most successful
programs to date have been in areas peripheral to its degree programs,
in remedial work in basic subjects and in off-campus programs (see Addendum to this session).

A current experiment, centered on cable television, of the Day-
ton-Miami Valley Consortium was reviewed. This program involves two
communities in the Dayton area now being wired for cable. After an
educational marketing and demand study is made of these communities,
teams of faculty members from the area's colleges and qualified persons outside the colleges will work with technical experts and others to prepare courses of study to meet the expressed interests of
cable subscribers. This experiment should tell us a lot about the
potential audience for external study, the motivation and staying power of such an audience, the techniques of delivering programs over a
cable system, and the effectiveness of certain kinds of team-based
efforts to create programming.

Other large-scale projects were also discussed, including the PLATO computer-based project at the University of Illinois and the MITRE Corporation's system, TICCIT, which is based on both computer and broadband technology. The question was raised as to whether such experiments had anything to offer now to the educational community at large. Consensus was that all such experiments are still very much in the R & D phase and that their general adoption now, even if possible, would be premature.

Mention was made of one specific kind of program that might lend itself to widespread adoption now: the use of open circuit television (and ultimately of cable) for the in-service training of municipal employees, police, firemen, social workers, etc. At least one such program can now be seen in operation over Channel 31 in New York City, where instructional broadcasting for these purposes is done regularly. City employees taking this on-the-job instruction are, of course, tied to a broadcast schedule, but this does not appear to be a serious limitation. In small and medium size cities, it might be possible to achieve some flexibility with videotapes either to back up or to eliminate the broadcast schedule; but the logistical problems as well as the extra cost of preparing and distributing large numbers of videotapes should be examined carefully by any interested community.

The general import of the discussion from the panel and from the floor was that the transfer of technology to the teaching-learning process, a process that is itself but poorly understood, is in a very early R & D stage; that promising experiments are going forward in various technologies and in various kinds of institutions; but that the managers of urban institutions and of local governments are well advised to move cautiously in this area and only after thorough investigation.

During this panel session a rather complete case history of institutional experiences was presented. As noted earlier, NYIT has attempted many experiments in educational technology. As has been the practice in these panel summaries, we present experiences here to afford maximum dissemination of information that may be transferred to other institutions. (See Addendum to this session.)

In general, educational technology systems have been as well received on the campus as a long lost relative is by his family at the
reading of the will. Many of the reasons for this situation have been
heard before but the principal ones bear repeating: lack of faculty
incentives, threat to faculty jobs, innovation versus sound education,
and the disruption of a rather delicate balance of power. Despite the
publicity, notwithstanding the millions of dollars spent on hardware
and software, and ignoring the few instances of reported progress, the
fact of the matter is that technology has not made a significant impact on the campuses of institutions of higher learning.

Are the prospects altogether bleak for them to do so? Perhaps
yes, but, on the other hand, the simple economic facts of life will
generate ever increasing pressures to force the broader application
of educational technology, more as a means to an end than as an end
in itself. Put plainly, the slope of college expenses is far greater
than the prospective slope of income.   While inflation continues unabated, there is a saturation level for tuition -- a point of dimin-
ishing return -- which in effect poses a restraint that is hard, particularly for private colleges, to digest.   In this vein, it may be
presumed that the pressure for innovation will be far greater in the
private segment than in the public segment of higher education.   Although true costs per credit hour in state supported colleges far exceed those for most private colleges, the fact remains that from the
buyer's point of view the student tuition at the public colleges runs
no more than one-quarter that of the private colleges.   The anomoly
of two-thirds of the colleges in the northeast region of the United
States being private but containing less than one-third the student
population logically follows.

What is the conclusion? Simply put, college jobs are drying up
rapidly. It doesn't seem possible, but faculty members everywhere are
beginning to realize the pyrrhic victory, so painfully achieved, of
teaching far fewer hours for more pay. What good is such a status if
it is at best ephemeral?

BIBLIOGRAPHY

Armsey, James W. and Dahl, Norman Co., "An Inquiry into the Uses of Instructional Technology," Ford Foundation, 1973.

Carnegie Commission on Higher Education, "The Fourth Revolution; Instructional Technology in Higher Education," McGraw-Hill, 1972.

Levien, Roger E. (with chapters by S. M. Barro and others),"The Emerging Technology; Instructional Uses of the Computer in Higher Education," McGraw-Hill, 1972.

Oettinger, A. and Zapol, N.,"Will Information Technlogies Help Learning?", Teachers College Record, pp.5-54, September 1972.

Sloan Commission on Cable Communications, "On the Cable; The Television of Abundance," McGraw-Hill, 1971.

Tickton, S. G., ed., "To Improve Learning; An Evaluation of Instructional Technology," Report of the Commission on Instructional Technology, two volumes, R. R. Bowker Company, New York, 1970.

ADDENDUM

During this panel session, the experiences of NYIT, a college which has attempted many experiments in educational technology, were recounted. As has been the position of these panel summaries, we present this information here to afford dissemination of actual experiences that may be transferrable to other institutions.

Dr. Theodore K. Steele, Vice President for Academic Affairs at NYIT reported that even though they had had their share of disappointments, there had been successful application of educational technology to the learning process as based on the premise that teaching is only one of several means of effecting learning.

The major portion of successful application occurred in the areas of remedial programs for underachieving high school graduates and off-campus programs both in the corporate colleges and the military services.

In the former area, educational technology vehicles such as linear programmed texts, scrambled texts, audio tapes, teaching machines, computer terminals, single concept films, video tapes, and the old fashioned lecturer and tutor have been used. Differential pacing was allowed for in such programs as introductory mathematics, transitional physics, introductory college composition, and reading improvement since the student population varied considerably in achievement. In some instances, even students with good high school records enrolled in these courses because they had never studied physics, for example, which is a prerequisite for science and technology degree studies. Through various educational technology devices, such students can accelerate rapidly through the prescribed material and very often can challenge successfully the corresponding first college level before the end of the semester. Notwithstanding the relatively high cost of computer-based educational systems, (it has been estimated that the conventional system of education is cheaper by a factor of ten compared to the most optimistic computer based systems) they do represent an imposing technology aide.

Simple systems such as the NYIT Educational Management Information Systems (EMIS) can be utilized at reasonable cost. The NYIT EMIS system for introductory physics has proved both useful and economical in improving individualized education. In essence, this system utilizes the computer in the least expensive manner by putting into the CPU the minimum possible information. The student is equipped with workbooks and problem books tied to keywords stored in the computer. BASIC language is utilized, simplifying the communication problem from teacher to computer. By providing a random selection of keywords for both exercises and examinations, a reasonably secure system evolves. The computer maintains an accurate, constantly updated profile of the sutdent's progress and will control his movement through the course should he fail to meet prescribed minimum levels for any particular segment. Of course, textbook reading assignments, supplementary problems, live and simulated laboratory experiments, together with tutorial sessions round out this teaching strategy.

Very shortly, the entire basic three semester college physics sequence at NYIT will be on the EMIS system. The several hundred students who have already completed their studies via this system either matched or outperformed students following conventional routes.

EMIS systems for basic mathematics and college composition are nearing completion. It should be noted that the EMIS system suits quantitatively oriented courses far better than qualitative expository courses. Needless to say, NYIT does not inhibit any humanities faculty member from exploring the possibilities of EMIS or any other system.

The area of off-campus education, particularly at the corporate colleges and military bases, has proved to be an effective outlet for innovative educational systems which have included some sophisticated technology. Here it must be admitted that NYIT is dealing with a more mature and highly motivated student population, who know what they want and will move with alacrity to achieve it. The various educational modes include the liberal use of independent study packages, weekend seminars, lectures dovetailed to work experience and company educational programs, audio tapes, WATS line tutorial sessions, video tapes, facsimile transmission, on-campus intensified seminars of one or two weeks, telewriter systems, as well as computer terminals. The success achieved at the NYIT Eastern Air Lines Management Program and its Management and Technology Programs at the Signal School at Fort Monmouth, although on a limited basis to date, has encouraged broader excursions into this mode of education. The importance of the communications and management procedures cannot be overemphasized, nor subordinated to the educational process itself.

The success of NYIT's continuing education program, with its innovative technological resources, may be measured by the fact that its student population has burgeoned from 300 to almost 3,000 over the past three years. As for cost, tuition for these students is roughly 60% of that for conventional on-campus students. The application of individualistic and technological strategies plays a dominant role in reducing fixed costs. Like it or not, it is an established fact of life that the teacher is still the most expensive cost item, albeit a necessary one, in the college budget.

What about the scene on the campus? Just summarizing a few of the educational technology strategies employed by NYIT over the past nine years, it is safe to say that the downs <u>do</u> outnumber the ups. One system clearly on the negative side was a two-year experiment using computer aided instruction via an IBM 1500/1800 computer system for a course in basic computer technology. After 500 students had passed through the course, it was concluded that the experiment was an educational success but a financial failure. The cost ratio was hardly as bad as suggested above, but certainly nothing to sing about.

Virtually all of NYIT's advanced computer technology courses are all or partly on terminals with clear indication of costs being no greater than those involved in using conventional teaching systems. The cost curve slope is downward as larger numbers of students are assigned to the increased number of terminals now available.

The use of teaching machines for courses in electrical and electronic circuits did not pan out too well primarily because of marginal software inputs and a cumbersome delivery system. The basic function of the teaching machine was to turn pages electromechanically. Branched program instruction books, in essence, do the same job without taxing the patience of even the most motivated student.

Televised courses in history, mathematics, economics, reading techniques, and literature (among others) proved to be universally unpopular, although most economical. It seems safe to conclude that the average student has a threshold tolerance of 20 minutes perhaps before his mind wanders when watching a canned TV lecture. It has been found that it is necessary to introduce some mode of interaction between the student and the technology vehicle to sustain his interest. Witness the popularity of the computer terminal where a continuous dialogue is maintaintd between student and machine.

VI. FIREGROUND COMMUNICATIONS TECHNOLOGY

RAYMOND C. PICARD, CHIEF

Huntington Beach Fire Department
Huntington Beach, California

PROBLEM STATEMENT

A light, highly portable means of sending and receiving voices on the fire scene between firemen (optimal) or at least between fire officers and their crews
(minimal), particularly between fire fighting personnel inside and outside a burning structure is urgent-
ly needed.

BACKGROUND

Effective fire fighting operations, as well as the safety of the
fire fighting personnel, depends to a large extent on communications
between members of a fire fighting team. Fireground communications
largely consist of voice, hand signals, and hand held radio devices.
The latter are used primarily by officers since fire fighters must
have their hands free for their work in controlling fires.

There are a number of conditions at the scene of a fire that inhibit traditional forms of communication. These conditions include
(1) noise caused by the fire, by fire fighting apparatus, and by the
crowds that gather to watch; (2) restricted visibility due to smoke
or nighttime darkness; (3) physical barriers to communications between
fire fighters; and (4) the large number of persons potentially involved
in the communications network.

Fire fighting is a team effort requiring coordination among team
members. From the moment the first fire engine arrives at the scene
of a fire, the need for clear communications is critical. The man
charged with connecting the hose to the hydrant must be told when to
open the hydrant. This seems like a simple matter, but hydrants are
often out of the line of sight or otherwise obscured from the pumper
operator[1].

When the fire is being attacked, fire fighters advancing the hose
lines and those who are ventilating the building must be able to communicate. If a building is opened before water is available, the fire
may get out of control before it can be suppressed. It is also important that fire fighters inside a building be able to communicate
with each other and with the command posts. They need to be able to

report sudden shifts in the progress of the fire and to call for assistance when needed. Communications inside burning buildings are
severely impeded by smoke and face masks of the necessary breathing
apparatus.

> It is apparent that communications have a very signif-
> icant impact on the utilization of manpower. We are
> dealing here with an emergency situation in which
> there can be many changes in a short period of time;
> these changes require changes in manpower assign-
> ments. If this group of fire fighters fails to re-
> pond quickly to these changing conditions, the fire
> may quickly get out of control or at least spread to
> an extent that requires many more personnel.[1]

A special problem in fireground communications is that of the
high-rise building fire. Not only is communication more difficult because of the possible increased distance from the command post to the
fire, but the building structure itself interferes with radio communications. This is particularly true when communicating from the inside of the building to the outside.

The development of an appropriate communications device and system, capable of effectively functioning under the above conditions,
would improve firefighting effectiveness and safety. All firefight-
ers, not just officers, should have communications capability.

PANEL SUMMARY

The importance of this need has been exposed on at least three
occasions. First, the 80 cities participating in the NASA/Interna-
tional City Management Association Technology Application Program had
ranked this need as second among the top 15 priority problems selected from the list of 469 problems. Second, a 1972 National League of
Cities poll of municipal fire departments showed that communication
devices used at the fireground were ranked third in dissatisfaction
among 10 types of fire equipment. Finally, the Public Technology, Inc.
conference on innovation in the fire service, held in December 1972
in New Orleans, again uncovered this need, particularly as related to
fighting high-rise building fires.

There have been many instances at fires in subways that have re-sulted in death and injuries to fire fighters and the public. During 1972 and 1973 there have been 20 to 25 fires in Boston subways. In one case alone, the fire caused one death, numerous fire fighter in-juries, and forced the evacuation of 400 people from the hot and smoky underground tunnel. Fire loss was over $250,000.

The major tactical problem encountered was delayed fire depart-ment attack due to poor fireground communications. There were practi-cally no radio communications between the ground forces and the sub-way fire fighters. This was true even though there were ample walkie-talkies and multiple radios available. The real problem is the ina-bility of portable radios to transmit through ground or structural ar-eas, even at close range.

While working under these extreme emergency conditions, Boston command officers partially solved the communication problem by relay-ing radio transmissions through portable equipment stationed at very close intervals throughout the tunnel.

Problems on the fireground have also occurred in Boston due to portable radios getting wet and freezing. Background noises have also created difficult situations. Many fire chiefs agree that portable radios should not have to operate only under dry conditions. Elimi-nation of the hand held equipment requirement is also desirable.

One possible solution to the problem might be the use of portable radios operating through mobile repeaters. Low-powered portable units can trigger higher output mobile units to relay the signal to distant locations or to penetrate buildings and subways.

Voice communications are on the increase in the fire service and modern fireground management dictates a strong command posture. The most effective method of achieving these objectives is to establish a strong communications network between all personnel. Because attack personnel operate away from their apparatus, fire fighters must be equipped with quality portable radios. It is obvious from case his-tories that portable radios have not been developed to the point that they are fully effective and reliable on the fireground.

If and when the portable radio problem is solved, discipline on the use of radio and air time still must prevail. Many times, through technology, the scientist provides a solution but the user does not know how to use the product. If everyone on the fireground is issued a portable radio, air time could be saturated. Common sense and reasonable use must prevail.

There are three principal problems in fireground communication:

1. Lack of suitable equipment for the fire service. The fire service has been using general purpose portable radios. They are designed for the general market, rather than for a specific fire service use. The fire service must acquire from the private sector a radio that is rugged, reliable, inexpensive, and operable for a considerable period of time under fireground conditions.

2. Fire service portable radios have not been miniaturized. The aerospace industry has developed the state of the art to the point that miniaturization for the fire service is possible. The problem is that it is not yet available to the fire service in quantity. Fire fighters should not be encumbered with hand held or bulky portable radio units.

3. Portable radios are not designed to operate under fireground noise conditions. Fire fighting operations have high ambient noise levels which drown out the conventional microphone or speaker systems. Equipment must be developed that will permit the fire officer to give and hear instructions over the portable units which are inundated by fireground noise.

Another desired feature would be the development of a fireground personnel-radio locator system. Fire fighters trapped or in trouble could activate an emergency unit and rescue forces, using range finders, could then home in on the signal and free the fire fighters.

There is a strong need to solve the fireground radio frequency problem. Some departments have the exclusive use of channels and others are assigned to groups of departments. There are many complaints of overcrowded frequencies throughout the United States. Many departments do not use multiple channel radios with a mutual aid frequency. When major fires occur that require support from other fire forces, confusion generally prevails.

Telemetering of signals from fire companies to dispatch centers are just coming into use. Generally, this method is used to reduce air time and change the status of the vehicles automatically in the communications center. More equipment of this type needs to be made available at a reasonable cost.

Private companies selling general use portable radios frequently focus their full attention on the production and sale of their units rather than investigating the real needs of the fire service; that is, to develop a light, compact, rugged, and low-cost fireground portable radio.

Industry has stated many times that they will be responsive to the problem of the fire service if they could get a firm equipment market need. Over the past 10 years, one corporation reported that they have received requests many times to modify radios for installation in fire helmets. However, the quantity on any one order has been small. This makes the unit price high and causes the user to shun the product. Industry's view of what the fire service wants is as follows:

> Install a fireground portable radio in a fire fighter's helmet in such a manner that it would not increase weight or impair its safety function.
>
> One or two watt capacity radios that can penetrate high-rise structures and subways and would have a range of at least one mile.
>
> Microphones must not interfere with face masks nor create breathing problems.
>
> Permit a fire fighter to hear and transmit in high ambient noise areas but still not interfere with his ability to detect sounds and conversations in the immediate area.
>
> A push-to-talk switch that is readily accessible.
>
> Batteries that will last for at least one hour of high-use time.
>
> Cost should be in the $200 range.

Cost is one of the major problem areas. Current state of the art radios meeting the above criteria cost abour $800 to $1,000.

New technology is generally being used to add features to the radio, rather than reducing the cost, weight or size.

Public Technology, Inc. has been working on a fireground portable
for some time. Their goal is to locate, or cause to be developed, a
low cost, reliable high use unit. Analysts suggest that the equipment should operate in the ultra high frequency (uhf) range for pen-
etration.

One of the current projects is to determine if the scientific
breakthroughs discovered by NASA can solve some of the fire service
problems. Their unconventional design techniques would reduce circuit
size, improve electrical performance, and selectivity of channels. It
is hoped their design will lower the cost of the circuitry and improve
durability.

The modular construction would allow for longer life and easier
maintenance. This technology has had little public use to date.

Public Technology's User Design Committee has suggested the following constraints for a short-range fireground communications device:

1. The device should be completely enclosed in some regular part
    of the fireman's equipment, possibly his helmet (if it were
    to be redesigned for space and safety consideration), or his
    life support system.

2. The device should be workable without use of the fireman's
    hands once he is on the scene; for instance, it would be im-
    possible to manipulate a device while handling a 1½-inch hose
    or climbing a ladder.

3. The device must be relatively light, especially if it were
    to be located within the helmet; e.g., the helmet is of a
    polycarbonate construction weighing from 12 to 16 ounces.

4. The device must be able to function under extreme variations
    in temperature, e.g., from -20 to +160 degrees.

5. The device should have a range of 1,500 feet and should have
    the capability of transmitting messages through structures
    of masonry, brick, or steel beam reinforced concrete con-
    struction.

6. The device should be reasonably priced.

7. The communications links should be sufficient to include all
    operating personnel on the scene requiring communication yet
    provide for communication with individuals.

8. Consideration may be given, if necessary, to redesigning the
    basic fire support equipment to accommodate the communica-
    tions device.

It is perhaps best to close this developmental topic with the above suggestions. It is useful to point out that sessions such as these working groups, certainly, over the long run, heighten awareness of these typical, somewhat mundane, but nevertheless vital problems, which are facing the urban sector.

REFERENCE

1. Newman, James M. and Irving, George F., "Modern Technology in the Fire Service," Institute for Self Government, Berkeley, California, 1973, pp. 91-92.

VII. POLICE VEHICLE TECHNOLOGY

DAVID R. POWELL
U.S. Department of Justice
Washington, D.C.

PROBLEM STATEMENT

Develop specifications for police vehicles so industry can view them as a new market, independent of present automobiles.

A. INTRODUCTION

Officer Jones is parked at an intersection in the north end of town watching for red light violations. He's assigned to accident investigation and because there's a freeway on his beat, he's been issued a "special" police car.

It is a plain sedan, but features a fully loaded engine, weighted frame, positive traction rear end, heavy duty siren, radio, emergency lights, springs, etc. Jones has heard all these terms but doesn't fully understand what they mean, except that he's got to idle to keep his radio turned on and it is almost impossible to keep the car from overheating.

A speeding car passes and Jones pursues. A high speed chase develops. Radio dispatch advised that he's chasing three armed men who

are fleeing a bank robbery during which a teller was shot. Jones' decision to continue the chase is clearly justified, but his problems
begin.

First, the radio is mounted too far to the right (for a nonexistent partner) so Jones can't change channels or replace the mike in
its holder. Jones puts the mike down on the seat, but the spring-
loaded mike wire is too short and keeps dragging the mike off the seat
onto the floor. He's forced to drive holding the mike in his hand.

Jones wisely slows down at each intersection. Soon the brakes
begin to fade. There is no horn ring, so Jones has to grasp the wheel
in his left hand and operate the siren by poking at the horn button
which his left elbow. Periodically, the mike wire twists itself around
the steering column as Jones struggles with the wheel through sharp
turns.

A suspect shoots at him and Jones draws his revolver. He immediately realizes his mistake because there's no way he can use it in
the middle of a chase. The trouble now is that his clamshell style
holster requires two hands to reholster the gun. He's forced to lay
it down on the seat, and soon it is on the floor, under the right seat.

The suspects drive into a fairly deserted industrial park where
Jones can use his engine power to full advantage. When he is 20 yards
from success, the wiring system catches fire and shorts out. The car
stalls and quits. Jones manages to get off one last radio message
describing his situation. This results in a later reprimand for using language prohibited by FCC regulations.

This is an easy story to remember because it really happened.
In spite of considerable advances in police vehicle technology, we
still don't seem to have been able to get it all together.

B. IMPORTANCE OF THE PROBLEM

The importance of the problem is underscored by the 1972 National Bureau of Standards (NBS) survey (done for the Justice Department's
Law Enforcement Assistance Administration - LEAA) that showed police

vehicles as the number one equipment research concern of 1,500 United States police departments, representative of all sizes and regions. It also provided the basis for the educated guess that there are about 160,000 police cars in use in the United States. Of these, 84% are standard four door sedans.

More than half of these vehicles are in service 17 to 24 hours a day. Especially in the cities, they are driven by three different people each day. For this fact alone, one can sense the difficulty of finding a design of any aspect of a police vehicle likely to satisfy everyone.

This problem statement will deal with a few select areas of concern. No attempt will be made to offer solutions. The intent is to establish a framework for study from a variety of perspectives in the public and private sectors.

The problem areas that we will concentrate upon will be (1) police vehicle economics, (2) the man-machine interface, (3) industry and the police vehicle, and (4) the group-machine interface. We will grapple with the everyday practical problems, but will also let our imagination run a little with some ideas that may someday deserve exploration.

1.   Police Vehicle Economics

As pointed out above, the recent NBS survey indicated that there are about 160,000 police cars in the United States. Roughly half of these are purchased every year at from $3,000 to $4,000 a unit. This represents close to $300,000,000 of business to the automobile manufacturers in unit sales alone, and conversely a substantial bill for the taxpayer. This figure, however, represents only a small part of the investment required. We must view the economics of police vehicles from the larger perspective of life-cycle costing against the value received.

This raises many complex issues, only a few of which can be mentioned here. The same NBS survey reported that 62% of police vehicles are out of service for repairs almost three days each month, and the

remainder up to five days. The most serious maintenance problems reported by the large cities centered around a shortage of mechanics
and problems with brakes and engines. Ninety percent of the 1,500 police departments polled reported less than 12 miles of use from a gal-
lon of gasoline.

G. Ray Wynne points out in his book, "Police Transportation Management" that any consideration of life-cycle costing must start with
the resolution of several policy issues. These decisions are usually
the ultimate responsibility of general purpose government leadership.

It is probably fair to say that these leaders are most heavily
influenced, (or at least pressured) by purely economic considerations.
This gives rise to the first issue: How wise is a policy where the
firm that submits the lowest bid should receive the contract? Wynne
believes that a more balanced perspective can be achieved by first
developing policy restrictions that form the parameters within which
to consider questions rising from the following:
- Police vehicle use and deployment
- Take-home car use
- Numbers and types of vehicles to be purchased
- Vehicle pooling procedures
- Standardization
- Consultation with vendors
- Maintenance and repair procedures
- Fuel and routine operating costs
- Replacement
- Long-range programming

Once these policy questions have been resolved, it is then pos-
sible to judge the limits within which all elements of life-cycle
costing can be judged. Most of these are in the nature of performance
versus economy tradeoffs. The kinds of elements to be considered are:
- Initial purchase
- Maintenance arrangements
- Equipping the vehicle
- Vehicle assignment procedures

- Treatment of vehicles
- Facilities
- Tools
- Parts
- Mechanics' skills and work scheduling
- Gas, oil, etc.
- Resale

There are other problems not so directly related to the econo-metrice of police vehicles that are more complex and for which answers are not easily found. One of them is the relationship between the man and the machine.

2. The Man-Machine Interface

An important issue is that of safety. An early study done by the National Safety Council for LEAA's research arm, the National Institute of Law Enforcement and Criminal Justice, pointed out that "approximately three-quarters of police fleet vehicles are involved in accidents each year," and that "vehicle injuries constitute the most critical police problem." The latter may be an overstatement, but taken with the former, the implications are formidable.

No one can dispute that most motor vehicle accidents are due to human failure rather than mechanical failure. We will not deal here with the very cogent issues of driver training, and police management practices related to accident reduction. The issue to be discussed will center around the equipment with which the policeman must deal. When Officer Jones in the example described above was trying to drive with a radio mike in one hand, his safety was jeopardized. What are some of the basic safety issues?

The above-mentioned NBS survey pointed up some interesting facts:

1. Of the respondess, 75% stated there is a need for separate safety standards for police vehicles and 48% reported that at least one feature of police car equipment constituted a safety hazard. What are some of the safety features that need to be considered?

2. What do we know about the injury rates and characteristics? Would this kind of data help determine needs for padding, break-away handles, switch designs and the like?

3. What considerations need to be made of personal items of po-
    lice equipment which might affect decisions regarding the
    design of police vehicles?

4. What is the impact of the new federal regulations related to
    airbags, sequential interlocking ignition systems, 180 rear-
    view mirrors, and anti-pollution devices? Are exemptions in
    in order and feasible?

In addition to safety, there is the complex question of the need
for special equipment for police work. The NBS survey showed that
well over half of all police cars normally carry the following:

- a clipboard
- a fire extinguisher
- flares
- a first aid kit
- a shotgun
- batons
- blankets
- extra ammunition
- a brief case

In addition, state police cars usually carry riot control equipment.

The same survey indicated that most police cars require the following:

- a siren
- a mobile radio
- a public address system
- lights
- spotlights
- gun racks
- bubble lights
- mounting racks

Soon we will probably see the proliferation of computer equipment,
alarm terminals, and other devices to aid the flow of information for
emergency, as well as routine police business.

3.   Industry and the Police Vehicle

The other half of the spectrum lies in the private sector. What
can industry do to be more responsive to the needs indicated above?

The first issue is a complaint uncovered by the NBS survey that standard police vehicles lack sufficient room for police equipment. Modifications are necessary to fit everything in; a problem compounded by yearly design changes.

This has given rise to the complaint that there is not sufficient coordination between manufacturers of police equipment and police vehicles. Is this true? If so, what can reasonably be expected of the private sector and how can improvements be influenced by the public sector?

4. The Group-Machine Interface

How does the vehicle impact on the community? What might appear to be a simple problems -- how to mount a shotgun on a patrol car -- can have important community relations implications as experienced by several United States police departments.

There have been attempts to restore the policeman's individual relationship to a neighborhood, characteristic of the old foot patrol. Officers have been equipped with personal radios and smaller, lighter two-wheel and three-wheel vehicles have been employed.

Also, new color schemes for patrol cars have been introduced as a means to soften the militaristic appearance of the old black and white ones. But, is all this doing what was expected? Some claim that whether the vehicle is black and white, blue and white, all white, sedan or motor scooter, makes little difference; if there is uniformity, there is also autonomy, and public identification of the police as a semi-military unit rather than as individuals.

Some police administrators are moving in the direction of the general purpose patrolman upon whom is fixed much greater responsibility for such things as investigations, social service referrals, crime analysis, and a host of tasks designed to get the fullest measure of effectiveness from the man on the beat.

This idea is not new. The late August Vollmer, Chief of Police in Berkeley, California from 1905 to 1936, patterned his department according to these concepts. Among other things, his patrolmen used

their own family automobiles while on patrol. It was a sort of re-
verse take-home plan.

Each officer purchased his own car. The department supplied the
police accessories, gas and oil, and helped with the payments. The
officer usually modified the car to suit his own needs. The car was
easily identifiable as a police car by its outside accessories. But
the citizen, especially the youth, could recognize an individual policeman by name as long as he could see his car which was completely
distinctive. The officers reported that they felt somewhat special.
Is this a feasible concept, or would it pose prohibitive problems of
cost and fleet management? Might it be an approach worth exploring?

The above problem statement hardly begins to outline all of the
issues that need to be considered. It can serve, however, as a framework for studies that may lead to a more comprehensive understanding
of the complexities of police vehicle technology.

BIBLIOGRAPHY

"Analysis of Vehicle Breakdown Due to General Repairs and Accidents-
    A Report to the Detroit Police Department," Arthur D. Little & Co.,
    Boston, Massachusetts, 1970.

Babb, H. N., "Emergency Vehicle Operations Clinic," Police Chief, vol.
    39, no. 8, International Association of Chiefs of Police, Gaithers-
    burg, Maryland, August 1972.

Brinton, J. H. and Slott, I., Analysis and Evaluation of Philadelphia
    Police Department, Franklin Institute Research Laboratory, Phila-
    delphia, Penn., March 1972.

Byrd, A. P., "Motor Vehicle Management Study," Columbus, Ohio Police
    Department, September 1972.

Furr, R. P. and Dwyer, W. O., "Patrol Car Selection - A Systems-Anal-
    ysis Approach," Police, vol. 15, no. 10, Charles C. Thomas, Spring-
    field, Illinois, June 1972.

Ludwig, H. G., Study of the Police Patrol Vehicle-Detroit, Wayne State
    University, Detroit, Michigan, March 1970.

McCain, R. R., State Police Command-Management Seminar-Staff Studies-
    Seminar 4, University of Maryland, College Park, Maryland, 1969.

McCleverty, J. J., "Police Driver Training," FBI Law Enforcement Bul-
    letin, vol. 39, no. 5, Washington, D.C., May 1970.

"Mobile Displays Put Patrolmen On-line to Crime Date Files," Identi-
    fication Officer, Law International Association for Identification
    vol. 13, no. 11-12, November 1971.

"Police Manpower and Equipment Resources Study," Ontario, California
    Police Department, Ontario, California, November 1972.

Sweitzer, R. B., "An Evaluation of the Prince George's County, Mary-
    land Police Departments' Personal Patrol Car Plan," February 1973.

"Vehicle Location and Status Reporting System Project, Phase I - Final
    Report," Montclaire, California Police Department, March 1972.

"Vehicular Aspects of Police Gunfight Situations," Law and Order, vol.
    20, no. 20, October 1972.

Wynne, G. R., "Police Transportation Management," Coda Publications,
    Studio City, California, 1965.

Wynne, G. R., "Tomorrow's Police Car," Police Chief, vol. 36, no. 1,
    International Association of Chiefs of Police, Gaithersberg, Mary-
    land, January 1969.

Chapter 2

PROBLEMS: POLICY-INTENSIVE

Here we discuss those working groups where the technology is well developed and needs only implementation to realize its ultimate effectiveness. Policy, personnel, or politics are often inhibitors to such implementation. The urban sector is trained to deal with these problems and, in this context, the local government constituency functioned well on the panels.

Emergency health care delivery had been discussed in detail at UTC 2. Our purpose in presenting it again was to determine if improvements cited at the first session have been disseminated. The consensus was that the technology exists and that local administrators know what to do; however, the problem is one of implementation through careful policy planning. Thus, this problem area has a new dominant issue and is people-oriented rather than technology-intensive and can be classified as an internal policy issue.

The other problems identified as external policy problems at UTC 2 -- cable television and power plant siting -- remain so. Our purpose in discussing them again was to expose any progress. With regard to cable television, new difficulties have arisen with franchising. The economic viability of the system looms ever more important since the timeline to fully realize its potential grows with each passing year.

With the energy crisis, siting of new plants, coupled with other-than-fossil fuel technology for power generation, are more important than ever. Mechanisms for local community education must be developed along with the technology to insure ultimate implementation.

MEDICAL CARE DELIVERY SYSTEMS

JOHN G. VENEMAN

Bank of America Associates Center
San Francisco, California

PROBLEM STATEMENT

Develop policy and institutional constraints to better implement available technologies for emergency
medical care delivery.

A. INTRODUCTION

A long-standing concern in the United States has been to develop
and deliver the highest quality of health care services to all our
people at the lowest possible cost. An integral part of this total
system is the delivery of emergency medical services. It is also one
of the parts most neglected.

This is true in part because emergency medical services are essentially community efforts and the allocation of local revenues are
determined most often by political priorities. Statistically, the
need for a concerted national effort to meet emergency medical needs
is glaringly apparent. The stress is on national, rather than state
or local, for it is in this arena that the broad public policy initi-
atives can be made and implemented. The need is for public leadership
at the highest levels of government.

A sound but modest start has been effected by the recent passage
of the emergency medical services legislation by Congress which au-
thorizes the spending of $185 million over a three-year period for
planning, developing, and expanding emergency medical systems. This
effort, to become operational, must be budgeted and funds appropriated
and programmed. However, it remains to be seen whether the House will
concur in the Senate's action to override the President's veto.

The existing delivery system of emergency medical and health care
service, viewed nationwide, is inadequate to meet the needs of the con-

suming public. In general, it functions inefficiently and often in-
effectively. It has not taken advantage of newly developed techniques
and technology, nor has it attempted to break out of the confines of
traditional delivery systems. This may be, in part, due to financial
considerations but it is greatly due to lack of knowledge of advanced
systems that could be usefully employed with sound cost-benefits.

An estimated 10 million persons are injured each year. Emergency
room visits in 1970 were approximately 50 million, with a projection
of 100 million visits by 1985. Medical emergencies are our third largest disease, just behind cancer and heart disease. Yet expenditures
for emergency health care are only one-hundredth the amount spent for
cancer.

The facts easily point out the imbalance. Yet to take a positive
"pay off" look, a 10% improvement in the system would yield a savings
of $3 billion. The economics of cost-benefit ratios of improved, ef-
ficient health care delivery systems point decisively to the need for
expanded and directed efforts. A $3 billion savings in an industry
that currently is at $70 billion per year is a need too obvious for
debate.

Emergency Medical Services (ESM) is an integral component of the
total, complex health care delivery system. Conceptually, it represents a facet of the system which structures health resources for
rapid response delivery to anticipate and control unforeseen circumstances, inherent characteristics of any emergency situation.

The objective of an EMS system is a concentrated effort to reduce
disability and mortality probabilities of specific episodes, or distinct life safety events, in the continuum of health care.

An EMS system must be developed within the context of generating
maximum utilization of existing health resources for meeting EMS situations. The EMS design, therefore, will vary according to competing
priorities and available resources. EMS is inseparable from the total health care system; policy and program framework, financing, or-
ganizational mechanisms, facilities and equipment, and application of
technology is subject to the dynamics of the system.

B. THE PROBLEM

1. General

EMS has received considerable attention in recent years. The mortality statistics are high enough to frighten people. But we are dealing with a problem that is laced with politics, public and private, and in politics, meeting obvious needs becomes complicated.

Utilizing a simplistic approach, we must determine whether the delivery of high-quality emergency medical services is a national or local priority. If it is national, then a careful look at federal activities and leadership is in order. High-quality health care during the 1960s appeared to be very high on the list of national priorities and goals. Conferences were held, legislation passed, money appropriated, programs initiated, research advanced, and then it all seemed to have dropped from sight. The Congress passed legislation in July 1973 that would provide categorical grants to local communities to upgrade their EMS systems and to also support research in this area, but the measure was vetoed on the grounds that this is under state and local jurisdiction and that the federal government should not interfere.

If EMS should be exclusively within state and local jurisdictions, which is conjectural, what are the problems faced at these levels. Principally, they are financial and jurisdictional, with the political more or less superimposed. The financial problems are obvious, if the priority is high enough and the money available, something will be done. Jurisdictional problems are more complex. There is often no compelling reason to joint venture or cooperate in developing a coordinated EMS system because one political entity may feel subordinated to another; the person in one jurisdiction who handles the ambulance service is the fire chief and in another it is handled by a private service. One jurisdiction believes it has an ideal system so why put more strain on it or let it slip by sharing with another jurisdiction. The problems are replete, and unless a high sense of urgency combined with heavy political pressure is brought to bear, EMS will continue at whatever level it presently occupies on the local scene.

The local community is really where the action is. The hard core decisions are made at this level; is EMS a priority item, will the city council or town board buy it, what will it cost, who will run it, how do the doctors feel about it and will they cooperate, can the local hospital handle it or are new facilities needed, can para-professionals be integrated into the system or will the professionals resist, what are the true community needs, is there specific data available on trauma and morbidity to enable priorities to be set.

These are but a few of the very specific problems at the local level. They are highly politicized, and if one neglects this consideration, no system, no matter how good and desirable, will be acceptable.

2. Components

a. Medical Services

The following comprise a few of the major problems involving medical services:

1. Many hospitals with emergency room service do not have the full range of equipment and personnel required to provide comprehensive emergency medical service, as indicated by the American College of Surgeons hospital classification.

2. Many emergency rooms are not open 24 hours a day.

3. Many emergency rooms are understaffed or have no permanent staff.

4. Problems exist in determining the optimum number of categorical emergency facilities required by a locality or region.

5. The same problem exists in determining the optimum number and type of health manpower required to deliver specific levels of services.

6. Problems exist in determining the optimum number of mobile facilities and equipment for a given locality or region.

7. The related problem of medical manpower for the mobile facilities exists.

8. Decisions must be made relating to the optimum level of training required for EMS physicians, nurses, assistants, Emergency Medical Technicians, public safety personnel, and citizens.

b.   Transportation

This set of problems involves transporting medical equipment and personnel to the victim and transporting the victim to the emergency room.

1.   Many patient transport vehicles do not have sufficient space for the delivery of specific emergency medical services.

2.   In many cases the transport vehicles do not have the necessary equipment required to deliver specific emergency medical services.

3.   In other cases, transport vehicle attendants have had little or no training in advanced first aid or higher level EMT training.

4.   Problems exist in determining the optimum number and type of patients' transport vehicles and equipment required by a locality or region.

5.   Related problems exist in determining the number of EMT's required and the level of training needed to gain the best results.

6.   In many cases, vehicle location creates extended delay times.

7.   Other problems involve the optimum replacement and maintenance schedules for vehicles.

c.   Communication

This set of problems evolves around the communication systems' configuration and EMS integration capability.

1.   In most communities, central access to the ambulance dispatcher is nonexistent.

2.   In most instances, public telephones are of the pay-or-no-tone variety requiring the victim or finder to have the proper coins to make a call for help.

3.   The questions concerning the best configuration of radio transmitters and receivers, distributed between mobile units, stationary units, and the communications center have not been addressed in most communities.

4.   The question of telemetry equipment and its uses and requirements, is not addressed adequately in most places.

5.   In most cases, where public and private ambulances exist, procedures have not been established for determining who gets the call to ensure the best possible level of responsiveness.

6.   Lack of coordination and integration of multiple communication centers cause increased delay time in dispatching ambulances.

7. Lack of adequate communication may cause an emergency room to be unprepared for the arrival of an emergency victim.

8. Untrained communications personnel cause unwanted delays in establishing communication linkages.

3. Information Exchange

One of the largest gaps in the EMS field is the flow of information. Most would suggest that the technology exists today to implement almost any needed system. Excluding the political and financial barriers, how many policy makers at the local level are keyed in or aware of these advances. And if they are not, what information system can be devised to accelerate the flow of information and put local policy makers in communication. Can an information network be devised to cope with this problem? Is it important enough to the overall effort to bother with? Looking at the realities, should an information network be rational, regional, or statewide?

4. The Consumer or Client

A service system such as EMS to be effective must develop a clear and accurate picture of the market it serves.

1. Population age characteristics will determine if emphasis should be placed on cardiac problems.

2. Population distribution puts stress on transportation requirements if the dispersal is great.

3. Mobility of population often places the consumer in unfamiliar territory and away from his medical history records.

4. The consumer must be educated as to systems availability and how to use them.

5. Consumer needs should be delineated and system structured around them.

6. Consumer input is necessary to develop community support for EMS program.

C. OBJECTIVES AND GOALS

The objective must be the highest quality of emergency medical care delivered in the most efficient and effective manner. The goals should be acceptable and reachable in terms of what the local community or region can handle at any one point in time. Superimposition will not work, but if flexible models can be designed that any community can adopt and feel comfortable with, substantial progress will be made toward reaching the overall objective.

D. CONCLUSION

Some form of an EMS system exists in every community, at best in a sophisticated form or at worst, as a haphazard ad hoc effort. The challenge to public policy makers at all levels of government is to more effectively utilize their resource base, upgrade it, or if essentially nonexistent, to establish one.

Some questions which arise are:

What are sound alternative approaches to upgrading and improving EMS?

Can the EMS configuration be developed on an objectives-time frame-resource availability plan?

What can be done to encourage public policy makers at the national and local levels of government to upgrade EMS on their priority list and establish specific goals for performance?

What should the intergovernmental aspects of EMS be?

The questions are virtually endless but must be addressed. Conclusions are rather easily reached in a field where it is so very obvious that not enough is being done. It is hoped that the panel's activity will develop reasonable and necessary recommendations that can be implemented and directed toward some of the issues contained in this discussion.

PANEL SUMMARY

At UTC 2, the panel focussed attention on the transportation, i.e., response time, component of emergency medical care delivery. In this year's continuation the other important subsystems, communication and medical treatment (in the most general sense) were addressed. As suggested before and reinforced here, it is evident that the technology for adequate service exists. The various constituencies know their roles; the basic problem is still institutional and remains people-oriented.

The panel and audience in this working group highlighted many of the jurisdictional and financial questions. This summary will review these to see the roles suggested for the various governmental levels -- local, state and federal -- and for the essential institutions -- hospitals, physicians, private ambulance services, communications networks, the public and emergency service teams (fire, police). Two case histories will be presented to afford documentation in the hope that implementation in other localities will take place.

Let us first consider the roles suggested for the federal government. Congress is becoming aware of the problem of emergency medical care. Moreover, to assist in the development of antionwide services, regulations promulgating such services may be generated. The training programs provided by the Department of Transportation, which when coupled with a strong set of policy directions, can assure uniformity of service to all communities. Note that such regulations can also be brought to bear on the problems of equipment and the level of service standards.

State governments can act in a manner similar to that suggested for the federal government. In addition, it would seem that they have a great deal to do to develop logical regional bases for emergency services. Individual local governments generally cannot afford the entire cost or management of resources to cover an area which includes contiguous communities, but the state government has the opportunity to effect this on a regional basis using broad and strong standards.

In the end, however, it will be the local governments themselves which will have to provide the services (possibly in consortium with others). This means coordination of a host of institutions, all intimately involved in the system, and the development of appropriate tools for emergency treatment and delivery.

Let us review some of the ingredients to see what areas are an integral part of the overall system:

> Hospitals and physicians -- emergency room equipment, emergency vehicle equipment, interhospital coordination

Ambulances -- use of private versus public systems, designs, standards, training of crivers

Communications -- channels to be set aside, public access to services, training of operators

Related emergency services -- coordination with police, fire department, paramedics

Public -- awareness of need for emergency medical care, how to use system, how to help

While these are the easily identified areas, others surely can come to mind. Later, we will see how two cities have started to address these issues and to develop effective emergency care delivery. Before doing so, let us examine a major impediment to implementation -- lack of funds.

It was suggested that both federal and state governments must develop funding mechanisms to address this problem. Many programs do exist but local governments are not sufficiently sophisticated to gain access to them. In any event, the level of spending is well below the apparent need. Alternative means for financing must be fully explored. One suggestion made at the working group was to intimately involve the private health care insurance companies. Many studies have shown that good emergency health care is cost effective; this is, lives are ultimately saved and the number of patient days in the hospital lowered. Since the costs of hospital care are usually borne by the insurance companies, and this would represent a savings to them, such funds can be rechanneled into the improvement of trauma care.

A particularly important feature of this panel session was the discussion of two relatively new emergency health care delivery systems.

The first of these has been implemented in Southfield, Michigan which has a population of roughly 70,000. The object of this study was to improve, with whatever means available, their admittedly poor level of service. It was ascertained that the most significant life-saving measure at the scene of an accident was stabilization of the trauma victim. With this as the basic premise, it is clear that substantial revamping of their then-current practices was in order.

This meant the elimination of sedan-type ambulances and replacement by vans which can carry sufficient equipment for the necessary stabilization of the victim including EKG devices, fibrilation systems, and complete monitoring capability. There was provision made for constant communication between hospital and ambulance attendant to insure that the latter perform the requisite procedures. With this new equipment, the training of drivers and attendants became vital. The Southfield fire service decided to take on this responsibility. Through a screening process, 20 firemen (out of 67) were selected for the special program. An intensive 6-month, 360-hour course was instituted. These trainees were briefed by hospital administrators, doctors, nurses, etc. with constant updating and review. Moreover, each incident has been taped to provide critiques of the methods and techniques used so that everyone can learn from these experiences.

Measures of the effectiveness of this program have begun to be evident. Response time (although not by itself a complete measure) is now four to six minutes, compared to nearly twice that before inception of the program. At Providence Hospital in Southfield, the incidence of death-on-arrival is down 26% which suggests that their basic premise and its implementation are truly cost effective, and are saving lives.

The second program is being developed in Pinella County on the west coast of Florida. This 300-square-mile area contains roughly 600,000 people of whom 40% are located in St. Petersburg, 15% in Clearwater, and the remaining in smaller subdivisions. While this area has an abundance of private ambulance services, until two years ago, emergency service delivery was woefully inadequate due to poor coordination.

To improve the system, it was felt that a countywide approach would be best. Regulations were enacted to govern the training of ambulance operators, the standardization of equipment and ambulances (the sedan-type are still used). Communications developed through module telemetry are being phased in. Dispatching, a major coordination problem in the county, will be done through a single central office.

To assure overall coordination, a health planning council was formed to look into the three major elements of emergency care: communications, transportation (including accident-scene treatment), and facilities and services of hospitals. This task force includes electronics specialists, city administrators, physicians, hospital admininstrators, and community representatives. Thus all facets of the system are included to assure its vitality.

These two case studies, representing different approaches, suggest that since the technology exists we are dealing primarily with a policy issue and that almost any system will work. It will be necessary to track the various elements of all systems to see if common problem other than those identified here will arise in the future.

II.   CABLE TELEVISION

JOSEPH F. COATES

Office of Technology Assessment
United States Congress
Washington, D.C.

PROBLEM STATEMENT

Due to the complexity of providing cable television to communities, it has become necessary to provide guidance to local government officials, concerned citizens, and others as to what rational and effective procedures there are for coming to grips with this new technology.

BACKGROUND

Cable television has enjoyed many years of popularity in the countryside of the United States as a means of picking up and enhancing weak television signals to provide satisfactory viewing. In more recent years, however, television has begun to move into urban communities and cities where its unique technological potential will certainly go far beyond simple signal enhancement to improvement of reception.   The principal responsibility for managing cable is in the

hands of local governments against the background of state and federal regulations. As a new technology with major implications in the
community, the technical and economic choices confronting local governments are complex, and involve numerous trade offs and many subtle
implications for 10 to 20 years of development of that technology in
each particular community.

A recent report from the Rand Corporation, "Cable Television:
Handbook for Decision Making" (1) provides a convenient background in
its summary.

Cable television is a system for carrying television signals by
wire rather than transmitting them over the air. Instead of the 7 or
so television channels most Americans now receive, cable offers an
immediate abundance of 20 channels, with more to come in the future.
Cable television also holds the promise of immediate viewer interaction with the program source. These technical prospects offer many
undeniably dramatic possibilities, although some may prove to be more
dramatic than feasible.

Cable television began as a service to communities where conventional television reception was inadequate. Even now, cable principally serves small towns and rural areas where it can provide better
reception, more channels of broadcast television, and sometimes locally originated programs. These cable systems generally have been
highly profitable businesses.

Today, however, cable television stands on the threshold of development in the major metropolitan areas of the United States. Cable
systems in the cities and suburbs will differ greatly in technology,
economics, and services from systems built outside the major markets.
And contrary to what many people suppose, cable systems are unlikely
to be rich sources of profits and fees for cities, at least not in
this decade.

In time, cable television may influence the way we live as radi-
cally as the automobile and the telephone have done. Most individuals
and groups who have studied cable conclude that its growth will serve
the public interest. Still, the long-range effects of cable communi-

cations are largely unknown. The necessary and unavoidable short-term decisions that must be made will have long lasting, unforeseen, and possibly unintended consequences.

The development of cable television demands more decision making by local communities than most new technologies have required in the past. These decisions cannot and should not be left to federal and state regulators or to large, nationwide corporations and interest groups. Local interests -- business interests, local government officials, community group leaders, and individual citizens -- should have a voice in shaping the terms of a community's franchise, influencing its award, and determining the programming and services the system will deliver.

One can easily become fascinated with cable television as a new technology, but the programming it delivers is its real importance. Communities should focus on the services that cable can provide to people, not on the mechanics of the medium. Broadly speaking, cable offers five levels of improvements and new services:

> The same sort of programming we presently receive, but with higher quality pictures and some programs for more specific audiences.

> Pay TV, offering sports events, first-run movies, Broadway shows, opera, and the like for payment of an extra fee.

> Public access channels available to individual citizens and community groups. Often using portable cameras, all sorts of groups -- churches, Boy Scouts, minority groups, high school classes, crusaders for causes -- can create and show their own programs. With public access, cable can become a medium for local action instead of a distributor of prepackaged mass-consumption programs to a passive audience.

> New services to individual subscribers, such as televised college courses and continuing education classes in the home. Cable's capability for two-way communication between viewer and studio may in time permit doctors to participate in clinical seminars at distant hospitals, or enable viewers to register their opinions on local issues.

> New services to institutions, such as in-service training of nurses, teachers, and policemen. Public and private institutions might build their own two-way cable networks or lease channels to send x rays among hospitals, exchange computer data, and hold televised conferences.

The technical design of cable systems must allow for future uses as well as for those feasible today. However, urban cable systems face a real chicken-and-egg problem in providing more than better reception and a few more television channels. Until new services are developed, cable in the larger cities may not attract enough subscribers to warrant large-scale commercial construction. But until systems are built and large subscriber markets are assembled, new services will not be profitable. The result may be a slower pace of system construction in the major markets than some previous accounts have projected.

Because they use municipal rights-of-way, cable systems nearly always operate under a franchise from the local city, town, or county. At the federal level, cable television is regulated by the Federal Communications Commission (FCC). State regulation is also an increasing trend.

On March 31, 1972, a new set of FCC rules went into effect that changes the future course of cable development. The FCC rules permit all cable systems to bring in some television signals from other cities. At the same time, cable systems in the 100 largest television markets must provide at least 20 channels and must offer new nonbroadcast services, including:

> Local programming, usually known as "cablecasting," if the system has more than 3,500 subscribers
>
> Leased channels for pay TV and other services
>
> Public access to a cable channel
>
> A channel for educational programming
>
> A channel for municipal services
>
> A capacity for two-way services, such as public opinion polling, that require signals from the subscriber

The rules also require local franchise authorities to follow certain standards if their franchises are to obtain an FCC certificate of compliance without which the cable system cannot carry any broadcast signals. Franchise fees to the city, for example, are limited to 3% of gross subscriber revenues. In granting a franchise, the local author-

ity must consider the legal, financial, technical, and other qualifications of applicants by means of a full public proceeding affording
due process.

In effect, a local franchise authority cannot set more demanding
requirements than those specified in the rules unless it can justify
them to the FCC. This can be done by means of a special showing after a franchise has been awarded. However, the local franchisor has
full authority to define the franchise areas, set rates for service,
determine whether the system will be publicly or privately owned, and
select the franchisee.

Local decision making for cable television is a continuous process, moving from planning through drafting the franchise, selecting
the franchisee, regulating the system, and managing public services
on cable. It is also part of the overall local political process.
Many individuals and interest groups in the community will want to
inform themselves on the issues and make their voices heard.

With growing public awareness of cable, ownership will perhaps
be the most emotionally charged topic a community will confront. The
basic ownership issue is whether the community should follow the standard pattern of franchising its cable system to a private operator.
Other possibilities include municipal ownership, a public cable authority, noncommercial, ownership, or a joint venture between a commercial and a noncommercial group. These alternatives offer prospects
of greater community control and direct use of surpluses if the system is successful, but they also involve significant risk and demand
a much greater community commitment. On a national scale, public or
noncommercial cable systems would serve as useful yardsticks to measure the performance of private operators.

Two basic approaches, negotiation and competition, have been used
in cable planning and franchising. Under the first, the city selects
a prospective cable operator and negotiates the many terms and conditions that will go into the franchise. In contrast, the competitive
bid and award approach involves a longer and more formal proceeding

in which the franchise authority must detail the terms and conditions of the franchise in advance. The authority then invites bids from all interested parties and makes the award according to preestablished criteria.

Neither approach is clearly preferable to the other for all communities. Moreover, a combination of open competition and negotiation may be preferred. The Rand Handbook describes the competitive bid approach more fully, so that communities can be familiar with the steps it may entail. In cases where franchising authorities prefer stronger elements of negotiation, some of the steps in the competitive process could be eliminated or compressed in time and scope. These steps include:

1. Adoption of procedures for planning and franchising

2. Assessment of community needs, objectives, and alternatives

3. Public hearings and tentative decisions on major issues such as ownership, franchise district boundaries, and interconnection

4. Hearings on and adoption of a draft franchise document describing the general terms and conditions of the final franchise

5. Preparation and dissemination of a request for proposal from franchise applicants, based on the draft franchise document

6. Hearings on proposals received from applicants for the franchise

7. Decision on award of franchise

8. Application for an FCC certificate of compliance

9. Monitoring system construction and certifying performance

10. Continuing administration of the franchise

Citizen participation should be encouraged throughout the process. The franchising authority will want to consider forming citizen groups to advise it on issues such as ownership, public access, and use of the education and local government channels. The authority also will want to consider its need for community surveys, consultant assistance, and independent studies.

The FCC has mandated one cable channel for education, one for local government, and one for public access in the major markets. The
cable operator is to furnish these channels free of charge on an experimental basis for at least five years. Communities outside the major markets may also require such access channels in their franchises.

Simply making channels available, however, by no means guarantees
that they will be used well or even used at all. A community therefore should start drawing its plans to use the access channels early
in the decision making process. Public services on cable can include:

> In-school instruction
> Instruction for homebound and institutionalized persons
> Preschool education
> High school and post-secondary degree courses in the home
> Career education and in-service training
> Community information programming
> Community information centers
> Municipal closed-circuit applications

The most important reason to experiment now is to assure that public
uses of cable are not foreclosed by a rapid development of entertainment and other commercial services. Consequently, civic leaders, educators, and local officials should take seriously their mandate to
develop applications for the access channels in the next five years.

The Cable Television Information Center, established at the Urban Institute in Washington, D.C. to serve the needs of local governments in this area, suggests the general procedure outlined below for
any city that plans to utilize cable TV. Their broad outline paral-
lels the 10 steps outlined above in the Rand summary.

I.   ORGANIZING PHASE

    A.   Develop Basic Understanding of Cable Issues
    B.   Select Mechanism for Study

II. STUDY PHASE

    A.   Establish Study Procedures
    B.   Identify Issues for Study

III.   LEGISLATION PHASE

    A.   Identify Legal Restrictions on Local Regulation, Fed-
eral, State, and Local Limitations

    B.   Establish Procedures for Writing and Enacting Ordinance
with Public Participation

    C.   Draft Proposed Ordinance

    D.   Enact an Ordinance

IV.   APPLICANT SELECTION PROCESS

    A.   Decide How to Select Franchise

    B.   Prepare Application Form

    C.   Develop Public Proceeding that Will Afford Due Process

    E.   After Franchisee Has Been Selected, Determine What Tasks
Remain before System Construction Begins

V.   SUPERVISION AND ENFORCEMENT PHASE

    A.   Determine Responsibility for Supervision and Enforcement

    B.   Develop Process for Operation of the Supervisory Body

        1.   Arbitrate Day-to-Day Disputes

        2.   Review Overall System Operation

        3.   Guarantee Compliance with Respect to Ownership and
Control

PANEL SUMMARY

This report will underscore some of the high points in the panel
session. No attempt was made to establish consensus, although on some
issues there was general agreement. The experiences of the Rand corporation drew attention to a number of factors that have become significant since the preparation of their series of studies. While they
are not gloomy, they are sobering. Prominent among them are:

1.   The changing economic and financial conditions of the country, including inflation, tight money, and the devaluation of
the dollar intensify the problems of cable TV development,
both for the cable industry and for cities franchising cable
systems.

2.   Cable's probability of success in cities is still uncertain,
in spite of the availability of distant signals, local orig-
ination, and pay TV.

3.   Faced with the current financial constraints, the industry
has less incentive to overbid for franchises.

4.   One source of difficulty in cable franchising is that citizens and public officials value future benefits more highly
than profit-seeking companies.

5. Two-way service may evolve much more slowly than many observ-
    ers thought just a few years ago. It was suggested that in
    the intervening years, before two-way cable service is avail-
    able, close consideration should be given to applications of
    the telephone system for feedback as some systems presently
    utilize.

6. Anticipated profits from entertainment services will probably
    not be a satisfactory base for public services in the major
    cities. But closed circuit institutional services may be a
    very good early bet for development.

7. Noncommercial uses must develop their own sources of funding,
    especially in view of the fact that software, that is, pro-
    gramming material, will be far more expensive than hardware
    in the long run.

The regulatory morass as a major problem of local government officials was pointed out. The recent 650-page report of the Federal-
State-Local Advisory Steering Committee to FCC on Regulatory Relationships was cited. This is available from the National Technical Information Service, Springfield, Virginia as Report PB-223-147 at $6.50.
On review, however, it has been found that even this is not a complete
catalogue of issues. But 29 areas in which questions frequently arise,
may be identified. These areas include those related to privacy, service, consumer complaints, etc. Consequently, in order to stay abreast
of regulations, one must now go well beyond any single source or document for advice.

On a somewhat pessimistic note, it was speculated that cable TV
might be the SST of the telecommunications industry. Many of those
characterized as technocrats see a broad diversity of single and two-
way services. The commercial exploitation around entertainment is the
most immediately promising base for development. A general prescrip-
tion for citizens and local officials moving into the franchising area
is to do the following:

1. Identify a single person in the city government who will be
    the visible responsible person for cable TV development and
    franchising.

2. Identify the areas which should be reviewed and researched.
    These may include economic, regulatory, technical or other
    matters.

3. Give that responsible individual the financial resources to
    hire the expertise necessary to answer the questions in the
    areas cited above in (2).

4. Travel about; see what's going on. There is a lot to observe.
5. It may be that a particular community will decide, quite pro-
    perly, to wait.

A key to cable TV is defining what you want.

It was pointed out that a recent FCC action giving the go-ahead
to domestic satellite services for 1975 (partly supplementing telephone services) has implications for cable by making possible long-
distance links efficient among cable systems. This could become a big
factor in the economic viability of cable. Compare this to the situation 20 years ago when regulator changes permitted the development
of broadcast television networks.

Regional and local interconnect was emphasized as a potentially
important factor in planning, designing, and operating cable TV systems. The economic base for present franchising tends to be too limited to fund a diversity of programming. However, if contiguous communities interconnected and cooperated on franchising jurisdictions,
they might achieve a scale of operation that would be mutually bene-
ficial. For example, communities and franchising areas adjacent and
contiguous to universities may be able to tie into that for their mutual benefit. Similarly, central city franchisers that may focus on
particular ethnic groups may build a broader base by being able to
reach out into smaller knots of those ethnic communities in adjacent
areas.

Engineering problems are relatively simple in interconnection.
They are not the obstacle to interconnects, rather the basic issues
seem to be institutional. One way for a community to begin to consider interconnect issues is to fund appropriate analyses on a regional basis, as for example, through a council of governments or an
ad hoc study group.

The standardization of equipment and cable systems might amel-
iorate many of the interconnect problems. This is thought now to be
likely in the near future. Currently, there is brisk competition among
6 to 12 organizations manufacturing such equipment. FCC is deliberately trying to avoid locking the technology down to one system. It

was suggested that the interconnect issue and the public access issue
(a topic not discussed in this panel) are the two largest red herrings
in the cable TV franchising discussion.

The panelists in this session seemed to agree on these three basic points:

1. Local governments can't hack it alone.
2. The content and function of the system become major issues
    along two dimensions. The first, the immediate versus the
    future or longer term use of the system. the second, the rel-
    ative immediately obvious fundable uses for cable versus
    the socially and culturally spectacular ones.
3. The question of how the system is to be paid for is vital.

The present FCC regulations and procedures were distributed and
a copy is appended to this section. It may be noted that the basis
for these procedures is that far too many cities are following seriously faulty processes in franchising. On the other hand, the FCC is
not a super franchising agency. It will not tell local communities
what to do; it will not insist on any particular procedures, provided
the community has made an effort to arrive at an informed decision.
The FCC accepts the notion of dual jurisdiction with primary responsibility at the local government level. It is prepared to give advice, but its experience is that generally it is approached too late
by local governments to be of optimal advisory value. It was noted
that few citizen groups come to FCC despite FCC's interest in inter-
acting with these groups. Its principal clientele are individual communities, broadcasters, and operators. It was suggested that a more
aggressive outreach program on the part of the FCC might overcome the
apparent indifference on the part of citizens. This has been done
successfully by other federal agencies.

Pursuing the apparent indifference on the part of citizens with
regard to the cable TV issue, it was estimated that at best the steps
from beginning to completion of the franchising process take three
and a half years. Such a delay is a severe test of the stamina of almost any citizen group since it does not have a direct financial stake
in the operation. The panel seemed to feel that a key issue is in-

forming citizen groups such as educators, minorities, etc., of their
real or potential involvement and that such techniques as newspapers,
open phone interviews, educational TV broadcasts are means of accomplishing this.

A different set of issues was raised dealing with the renegotiation of cable franchises in those cases where the local government
or citizens feel that they have not been adequately served. Two cases
were cited: Palm Springs, California, and Sommerville, Massachusetts.
Each, for different reasons, has started or completed renegotiation
of its contract. It was noted that the Rand Corporation recommenda-
tion that nonexclusive franchises be granted would provide one lever
to facilitate the renegotiation of contracts with unsatisfactory per-
formers.

The widely held view that cable TV is a natural monopoly is not
as strongly held by economists now as it has been in the past. Generally, a municipality has nothing to lose and something to gain in
granting nonexclusive franchises. For example, in New York, it is impossible to grant an exclusive franchise. It was also pointed out
that there is still no widely recognized procedure for initiating and
conducting the franchising process. Both the National League of Cities and the Cable TV Information Service, however, either have some
material relevant to this at hand or are in the process of preparing
fresh documentation.

The problem of where to find consultants was aired. The panel
pointed out that the New York State Conference of Mayors and the California League of Cities have published lists of consultants who have
worked with municipalities within their states. However, it was agreed
that no documentation was available as to quality control or evaluation of the merits of these consultants.

While there is no simple chart or table outlining various strategies and tactics for initiating discussions with franchisers, several
services are available to recommend particular techniques. The issues
focus on whether to go to bidding, negotiation or some mixed strategy.

Many seem to endorse the concept of "favorite nation clause in franchises." That phrase is shorthand for the notion that one incorporates in the franchise, a proviso that a city be entitled to any services provided to any other city franchised by the same corporation in that state. It was further suggested that another way to promote the healthful change and growth of the franchise system as new technology develops is to provide a mechanism by which either party -- the city or the franchiser -- can raise the issue of why don't we have? and if satisfactory resolution is not obtained, it be submitted to arbitration.

ADDENDUM

FCC Minimum Franchise Standards

In its February 1972 Cable Television Report and Order, 37 Fed. Reg. 3251 (1972) the commission adopted its first set of comprehensive minimum standards for franchises. The commission's regulations are not directly applicable to local governments, but rather require a cable television system to satisfy the minimum standards before receiving federal authorization to use broadcase television signals. As presently amended, the rules provide as follows:

SUBPART C - FEDERAL-STATE/LOCAL
REGULATORY RELATIONSHIPS

S76.31 Franchise standards.

(a) In order to obtain a certificate of compliance, a proposed or existing cable television system shall have a franchise or other appropriate authorization that contains recitations and provisions consistent with the following requirements:
   (1) The franchisee's legal, character, financial, technical, and other qualifications, and the adequacy and feasibility of its construction arrangements have been approved by the franchising authority as part of a full public proceeding affording due process;
   (2) The franchisee shall accomplish significant construction within one (1) year after receiving Commission certification, and shall thereafter equitably and reasonably extend energized trunk cable to a substantial percentage of its franchise area each year, such percentage to be determined by the franchising authority;

(3) The initial franchise period shall not exceed fifteen (15) years, and any renewal franchise period shall be of reasonable duration;

(4) The franchising authority has specified or approved the initial rates that the franchisee charges subscribers for installation of equipment and regular subscriber services. No increases in rates charged to subscribers shall be made except as authorized by the franchising authority after an appropriate public proceeding affording due process;

(5) The franchise shall specify procedures for the investigation and resolution of all complaints regarding the quality of service, equipment malfunctions, and similar matters, and shall require that the franchisee maintain a local business office or agent for these purposes;

(6) Any modifications of the provisions of this section resulting from amendment by the Commission shall be incorporated into the franchise within one (1) year of adoption of the modification, or at the time of franchise renewal, whichever occurs first.

Provided, however, That, in an application for certificate of compliance, consistency with these requirements shall not be expected of a cable television system that was in operation prior to March 31, 1972, until the end of its current franchised period, or March 31, 1977, whichever occurs first; And provided, further, That on a petition filed pursuant to S 76.7, in connection with an application for certificate of compliance, the Commission may waive consistency with these requirements for a cable system that was not in operation prior to March 31, 1972, until the end of its current franchise period, or March 31, 1977, whichever occurs first.

In adopting these minimum franchise standards, the commission explained its general philosophy in the area of federal, state, and local relations as follows:

177. Dual Jurisdiction. The comments advance persuasive arguments against federal licensing. We agree that conventional licensing would place an unmanageable burden on the Commission. Moreover, local governments are inescapably involved in the process because cable makes use of streets and wyas and because local authorities are able to bring a special expertness to such matters, for example, as how best to parcel large urban areas into cable districts. Local authorities are also in better position to follow up on service complaints. Under the circumstances, a deliberately structured dualism is indicated; the indus-

try seems uniquely suited to this kind of creative
federalism. We are also persuaded that because of the
limited resources of states and municipalities and
our own obligation to insure an efficient communications service with adequate facilities at reasonable
charges, we must set at least minimum standards for
franchises issued by local authorities. These standards relate to such matters as the franchise selection process, construction deadlines, duration of the
franchise, rates and rate changes, the handling of
service complaints, and the reasonableness of franchise fees. The standards will be administered in the
certificating process.

Perhaps the most important part of the franchise rules is a clause
that was added as a July 1972 amendment, i.i., the proviso that a franchise issued before March 31, 1972 need not be in strict compliance
with the minimum franchise standards. Accordingly, there are now three
types of franchises which were issued before March 31, 1972 and thus
need not comply with the minimum franchise standards at all. Secondly, franchises which were issued before March 31, 1972 to systems that
became operational after that date must be only in "substantial compliance" with the rules. Thirdly, franchises issued after March 31,
1972 to systems which became operational after that date must be in
strict compliance with the rules. The commission has handed down a
number of decisions defining "substantial compliance." Among the most
important are the following: CATV of Rockford, FCC 72-1005, 38 FCC
2d 10; Sapulpa Cable Television, FCC 72-1106, 38 FCC 2d 584; LVO Cable of Shreveport-Bossier City, FCC 72-954, 37 FCC 2d 1037. But since
the commission has handed down literally dozens of opinions involving
franchise issues, further study of other cases is essential to making
any kind of truly informed judgment.

III. POWER PLANT SITING

SEVILLE CHAPMAN

Director, Scientific Staff
State of New York
Albany, New York

PROBLEM STATEMENT

To try to find areas of general or compromise agreement as to the important issues and facts so that con-
structive resolution of issues can be attained.

INTRODUCTION

There are seven primary elements to the problem which are enu-
merated below:

1. Demand - If past history is a guide, requirements for electric power double every 10 years. Obviously, this rate of increase
will level off; just when is not clear. Power is used for turning the
wheels of industry and for commercial and residential purposes, and
it is clearly out of order to say that we don't need more power unless the question of new jobs is simultaneously addressed. The basic
issue then is "Just what should be the schedule for additional power
needs?"

2. Market - The market is generally in the population centers.
It costs money which means higher rates to consumers to transmit energy or power by railroad, ship, pipeline, or electric wires. Therefore, from an economics standpoint, power station location is ideal
when near or in the cities. This is clearly a problem in urban technology. Should or should not plants be located in or near cities?

3. Taxes - The city managers and taxpayers like the power stations nearby so that they can be taxed. Several hundred million dollars for one power station is an attractive tax base. What are the
consequences of the tax situation? (This issue has been discussed
and documented at length at the UTC 2 workshop on energy.

4. Public Resistance - The nontaxpayers usually want the power
stations somewhere else because they are smoky, or noisy, or unsightly
(none of these of necessity has to be true), or in the case of nuclear
power plants, the people fear an accident. (A Hiroshima explosion is
an impossibility, but an accident is conceivable although thus far,
there has never been a third party fatality from the nuclear power
generation industry.) What can be done about pollution? What is the

radiation hazard? Is the hazard from nuclear radiation greater or less than the hazard of not having power?

5. Fuels - Fuel must be gas, oil, coal, or nuclear fission at least for the foreseeable future. Commercial fusion power and solar power seem decades away. Gas and oil are both in short supply. Low-sulphur coal is in short supply in the eastern United States. Desulphurization of coal is a reality only in the laboratory. Nuclear fission reactors, including breeder reactors, produce wastes that must be monitored essentially forever (at least 1,000 years) or be launched, somehow, into the sun. What fuels should be used? Who should pay for the new technology which must be developed?

6. Pollution - All fueled power stations reject, as heat, the majority of the energy supplied to them and convert only a fraction to usable power. This result is an inevitable consequence of the second law of thermodynamics. Nuclear stations need about twice as much cooling as coal-fired steam stations. The importance of water for cooling is obvious since air cooling is much more costly. Some people call this thermal pollution; others call it thermal enrichment. Certainly, all power plants produce some pollutants (Sulphur dioxide, oxides of nitrogen, particulates, or heat). None of us likes pollution. What uses can be made of rejected heat? What levels of pollution are acceptable?

7. Approvals - All sites -- onshore, offshore, on rivers, or wherever -- require environmental impact statements, hearings and approvals. Obtaining approval is a real problem. There is legislation in some states (New York, for example has a one-stop siting law) and there is some federal legislation. More is expected. Companies, on the one hand, have tried to get approvals quickly before opposition crystalizes, and on the other hand, they have engated in substantial public education first before selecting a site. Neither tactic seems to work. The interval between the decision to build a plant and commercial operation might be a dozen years if things go smoothly. What can be done to make the approval process more effective?

PANEL SUMMARY

The panelists addressed the issues cited in the original problem statement. Some of these bear repeating here for the data they provide for the subsequent intensive study required. Before doing so, however, a brief overview of the current energy situation seems appropriate.

At present, approximately 500 billion tons of coal are judged to be reasonably recoverable and at current rates (if they mean anything) much of it would last a considerable length of time (centuries). The significance of the Middle East situation rests on the fact that we are now importing about one-third of our oil requirements (or at least were at the time of the conference). Imports influence balance of payments.

The sulphur dioxide requirements are quite restrictive since a significant part of most oil and coal is sulphur. Supplies of low sulphur fuel are very low in the northeastern section of the United States. All energy except sunlight comes to the northeast via pipes, ships, railroad or wires (in order of increasing transportation cost). There is no fuel souce locally except, perhaps, offshore.

Unfortunately it is not simple or convenient for power plants to reconvert to coal, e.g., a new building may have been built on the coal yard. Even so, removal of sulphur coal is not yet a commercial reality. In terms of oil prices, note that $5 to $6 per barrel was probably an economic turning point. If technology is developed for desulphurization or for strip mining which would include restoring the environment, it is believed we might get the energy equivalent of a barrel of oil for about $5 or $6. Within recent years the price in the Middle East had been about $2 per barrel, was raised to $3 and then to $6. (Shortly after the conferences costs of $8 were discussed). If such a technology were developed, it is conceivable that a price war could ensure. In the event that this technology proved out at $6 per barrel, then the Arabs might sell us oil at $5. However, it should be noted that while this is not quite an exact analogy, the Department of Defense spends many billions of dollars for weapon systems it hopes not to use. Thus, there may be precedent for developing coal technology that may not be used.

Nuclear options are looking more favorable and it is conceivable that the total societal cost for nuclear power could be less than for fossil fuel power. The rejected heat from power plants might have some utility if the plants were near cities. However, hazards are real although they possibly can be circumvented. For light water reactors, or preferably for high temperature gas-cooled reactors, the estimates of the probability of a catastrophic accident breaching the containment vessel is 1 in 100,000 per year. This degree of safety is far greater than in more familiar situations such as coal mining. In a few decades we might have as many as 1,000 nuclear power plants and this would mean one accident per century. Is this safe enough? Can we even define safety in this context? The breeder reactor will not come along until the late 1980s and won't be needed until 1990; fusion will not come before 2000. Neither should affect our considerations today which are more concerned with energy production and conservation for this decade.

It was noted that after two and one-half years, the Atomic Energy Commission has just issued an operating license for the Indian Point 2 power plant in Buchanan, New York, subject to the provision of cooling towers costing some $70 million with additional operating expenses of $460 million. Consolidated Edison of New York had only four working days to prepare their reply. Biological studies have been made and are being continued. It is the opinion of Con Ed that the evidence of harm to the environment was at best speculative and not positive. Only if it is definitely established that harm would be done to the environment did they think it justified to place the additional cost burdens on the customer.

Population growth, mechanization and technological advances in industry, architecture, and transportation as well as potential shortages of natural gas and gasoline make it inevitable that requirements for electric power will double sometime within the foreseeable future.

Siting involves not only new power plants but the replacement of old plants with larger ones. Criteria clearly call for minimum degradation of the environment with nuclear or fossil plants and correspondingly, whether or not the plants will be cooled by lakes, rivers, estuaries, the ocean, or the air. Cooling towers of 500 feet certainly are an intrusion on the environment. Should consumers bear all the costs? Economics are certainly very much involved. Attention should be devoted to total energy systems where power, hot water, air conditioning, and solid waste disposal are considered in an integrated way. The prime need of the utilities is a one-stop or one-step power plant licensing law so that the process of getting a power plant on line can be streamlined. (New York State adopted such a law in 1972).

It must be emphasized that 10 to 11 years are still required from the time the decision is made to build a power plant until it is on line. It is useful to briefly delineate the steps in this 10-year process. Studies of the site and radiological safety can take one and one-half to two years and require 11 volumes 7-ft. tall for the necessary reports. Another one and a half to two years is necessary for discussion of these reports. Then there are open hearings on the construction which can take from one day to several years. Eventually a construction permit is issued and work can begin. Then there are more reports. After several years when the plant is 95% completed, an operating license may be issued which may require significant back-fitting (Con Edison's situation at Indian Point 2). The whole process involves costly uncertainty.

It was felt, however, that history would show that in this decade we will resolve the electric energy question and that siting would be an integral part of the activity. Power companies should be pro-active, rather than re-active and that siting should be of high priority, addressed by strong impact statements. It is important to involve the public and interest groups in the early planning, discussion, and decision. What has become the public's business has been much broadened in recent times. Although governments are not well tuned to develop this policy structure, the people must be part of it. A series of flexible communication channels from power companies to government is needed on siting and land use. Significant efforts should be made to use technology to find early solutions, for example, standardization of all nuclear facilities so as to reduce lead times. Utilities should make great efforts on environmental impact statements to demonstrate that they are responsive to public questions and that they also develop their credibility.

The public's point of view was summed up by the observation that there was a great deal of cloudiness and jargon in the regulations and actions and that no one has time to read 11 volumes to get the story. As any newspaper editor can tell you, any story can be told in two takes (about 1.5 double-spaced typewritten pages). Actually, recognition of the significance of some of the technological-societal problems has been due to grass roots efforts by the public.

Technical questions on the efficiency of pumped storage (filling high reservoirs with water at night so that more hydro power is available at times of peak afternoon demand) and the economics involved were raised. Remarks from the floor and from the panel indicated that while pumped storage had an efficiency of only two-thirds, it did provide power at peak times when it might not otherwise be available.

The long standing issue of using electricity for space heating came up again. While only one-third of the energy in fuel was delivered to the space heating equipment by electrical means, pollution caused by burning the fuel was handled by well designed central power stations having high stacks to disperse sulphur dioxide, rather than by possibly ill maintained home furnaces which might typically deliver only 40 to 80% of the fuel value to the space to be heated. It was agreed, that, on balance, the case for general space heating by electricity was weak.

The utilization of waste heat has important bearings on the environmental and siting problems. We might typically consider using such heat to melt ice and thus open the St. Lawrence Seaway in winter, to raise fish by warming water with two plants side by side so the fish would not freeze if maintenance work was being done on one of the

plants. Other possibilities include placing cooling towers adjacent
to apartment buildings to utilize the rejected heat or to evaporate
water uphill for both power and drinking since it seems so expensive
to pump it up. Many of these engineering questions have just reached
a research and development stage, e.g., there is a plant on Long Island, New York which does enhance the shellfish yields.

The policy issues underlying these matters, as suggested earlier,
truly make up the heart of the power plant siting problem. How can
we make progress in the making of public policy on such matters? What
mechanisms can we invoke? How do the various concerned groups communicate with each other and with the policy makers and the technical
community? Although meetings like this provide some of the information exchange, other methods are also needed. New York's one-stop
siting law is encouraging. It was noted that Florida, as well, had a
sunshine law requiring meetings of all government officials to be open
to the public. Clearly more intergovernmental discussions among federal, state, and local governments are needed.

The experience in the state of Maryland which involved interaction between John Hopkins University and the state was recounted. A
year and a half previously their power plant siting law requiring a
two-year ecological evaluation coupled with hearings became effective.
As a result, plans for a nuclear power plant have been shelved and
some fossil plants will have cooling towers. Low sulphur fuel will
be used at prescribed times. The success of the TVA in dealing with
its constituency must be noted in this context.

Education of public officials in these complex questions was considered important. Generally, local or state governmental officials
do not like to be told what to do and would rather make their own decisions, which in fact they are obligated to do. Therefore, credible
information sources such as professional society expertise must be
available to them. It is not Nobel Laureates that are needed, but some
credible experts who can explain the issues in simple English. However, it is clear that decisions are usually made on a legal or political basis rather than on technical justification. Such a basis some-

times leads to an incongruous situation because standards for air quality are due to suits and the like. For example, if at the contemplated location, the air is unusually pure, one cannot build a power
plant there because doing so may degrade the pure air there to a level
judged to be perfectly acceptable; yet any degradation has been ruled
illegal. Thus, power plants can be built only where the air is already
as impure or more impure than the required standards.

The psychology of advertising and the creation of insatiable public demand, coupled to rationing of power must be a prime policy question. Organizations like the National Governors Conference, the National League of Cities, the United States Conference of Mayors and
the International City Management Association plus others should be
involved with the utilities. Utilities are surely not in a position
to decide on a rationing system, but city government, regional government, states, and federal agencies should be involved in considerations of selling power so that an artificial demand for power is not
created which can be used as justification for building more power
plants which result in still more environmental problems.

The style of societal interaction is an adversary relationship.
There are many jurisdictions mostly manned by people with inadequate
technical background. This is in part due to the professional technological community's self-imposed isolation. Many problems change
with time and the engineering community, whether it likes it or not,
had better learn to deal with such problems in addition to the more
tractable objective ones they are accustomed to. As an example, note
that a plant in Vernon, Vermont was initially designed for open cy-
cle (water) cooling but the operators were asked to install cooling
towers for summer use. Years later, their license called for continuous use of towers and in winter they have problems with ice forming
on the blades, etc. They have yet to see evidence that the winter fish
are adversely affected by water cooling, but the rules of the game
change as time goes along.

New institutional arrangements are clearly needed. The New York
State Assembly has established a scientific staff (currently the only

one of its type in the country) to bring scientific and technological expertise and perspective to the legislative process. The staff is small (five people) and is supported partially by the assembly and partially by the National Science Foundation. It both anticipates and reacts to requests from committee chairmen. The prime problem is not obtaining information, but rather summarizing it in a page or at most two, and in the proper context in plain English. It is necessary for people to talk with each other; some people will find the technical aspects easy (or difficult); others will think the same of the legal matters (what law should be amended, what should be regulated, what results should be obtained from tax modifications, etc.); to others, the political aspects will be foremost. Energy conservation issues are even now before the legislature.

With regard to insurance, it is felt by many that the government is subsidizing the power industry. If nuclear power is as safe as it is claimed why can't private financing for accident insurance be obtained? No very satisfactory answer emerged. It was suggested that very probably the insurance companies really were not in a position to evaluate the hazard. Certainly, there had been no experience of third party accidents on which to base an estimate of hazard.

Other governmental issues were touched upon, e.g., the support for various research areas, particularly coal. The cost of getting "four corners" coal (from the New Mexico, Arizona, Utah, Colorado intersection) to eastern markets is clearly important. Was there a better way than by railroad cars? While coal gas (carbon monoxide plus hydrogen) is easy to make, pipelines for methane have been used in pilot plants at an estimated price of about $1.25 per million Btu versus a recently controlled (now being decontrolled) price in Texas of 26¢. With this artificially low price the Federal Power Commission has created an insatiable demand for a fuel (natural gas) that no one can supply in adequate amounts; reserves are diminishing rapidly.

The adversary system is really quite fragile in this area. A better informed public, through the media, and a better informed government working together with the power industry seems the only way to bridge the gap between the technology and the user.

BIBLIOGRAPHY

Ball, R. H., Salter, G., Dole, S. H., Hammer, M. J., Frederich, B., Mooz, W. E., Papetti, R. A., Richards, G., "California's Electricity Quandry: II. Planning for Power Plant Siting," Rand Corp., Santa Monica, California, R-1115-RF/CSA, September 1972.

Berlin, H. G., Gill, K. D., Yarrington, H. J., "Power Plant Siting -- An Overview of Legislation," Environment Reporter, The Bureau of National Affairs, Inc., Monograph no. 15, vol. 4, no. 8, June 22, 1973.

Chapman, D., Tyrrell, T., Mount, T., "Electricity Demand Growth," Science, vol. 178, pp. 703-708, November 17, 1972.

DiBona, C. J., "The Administration's Plant Siting and Energy Policies," Public Utilities Fortnightly, vol. 91, no. 13, pp. 21-26, June 21, 1973.

Eaton, E. D., VonMeister, L., Davis, E. F., "Summary of Forum II Proceedings, "Power Plant Siting, National Academy of Engineering, April 1972.

Final Environmental Statement, Virgil C. Summer Nuclear Station Unit 1, South Carolina Electric and Gas Company, U.S. Atomic Energy Commission, January 1973.

Friedlander, G. D., "Energy Crisis and Challenge," IEEE Spectrum, vol. 10, no. 5, pp. 18-27, May 1973; no. 6, pp. 36-43, June 1973; no. 7, p. 26, July 1973.

Gordon, H. S., "Offshore Industry Ahoy!" Chemical Engineering, vol. 80, no. 17, pp. 62-66, July 23, 1973.

Grey, J., "The Race for Electric Power," Westminster Press, Philadelphia, 1972.

Gustavson, M. R., "Toward an Energy Ethic," Transactions of American Geophysical Union, vol. 54, no. 7, pp. 676-681, July 1973.

Hearings before the Subcommittee on Communications and Power of the Committee on Interstate and Foreign Commerce, U.S. House of Representatives, May 4-27, 1971, Serial 92-31,92-32,92-33, Power Plant Siting, Parts 1, 2, and 3.

Jopling, D. G., "Plant Siting at the Florida Power and Light Company," Public Utilities Fortnightly, Vol. 91, no. 13, pp. 27-31, June 21, 1973.

Katz, M., "Decision Making in the Production of Power," Scientific American, vol. 224, no. 3, p. 191, September 1971.

Laws of New York State, Chapter 385, An act to amend the public service law in relation to the siting and operation of major steam
electric generating facilities, (became a law May 24, 1972); this
was Assembly Bill 12255-A, and Senate Bill 9800-B (the latter being
the final version).

"Legislative Action: 1971 and 1972," Council of State Governments,
Lexington, Kentucky, 1973.

Lowe, W. W., "Creating Power Plants," Technology Review, vol. 74, no.
2, November 1972.

Meredith, D. L., "Nuclear Power Plant Siting: A Handbook for the Lay-
man," Marine Advisory Service, University of Rhode Island, Kings-
ton, Rhode Island, Marine Bulletin no. 6, revised January 1973.

Metz, W. D., "New Means of Transmitting Electricity," Science, vol.
178, pp. 968-970, December 1, 1972.

Miller, A. J., Payne, H. R., Lackey, M. E., Samuels, G., Heath, M.,
"Steam Power Plants to Provide Thermal Energy to Urban Areas," Oak
Ridge National Laboratory, Oak Ridge, Tennessee, ORNL-HUD-14, Jan-
uary 1971.

Mrak, E., Chairman, Assembly Science and Technology Advisory Council,
"Nuclear Power Safety in California," copy of report to California
State Assembly, May 1973.

Nelkin, D., "Nuclear Power and Its Critics - The Cayuga Lake Contro-
versy," Cornell University Press, 1971.

Novick, S., "Toward a Nuclear Power Precipice," Environment, vol. 15,
no. 2, pp. 32-40, March 1973.

Rom, F. E., "What Can Nuclear Energy Do for Society?", Astronautics
and Aeronautics, vol. 10, no. 1, pp. 56-61.

Weinberg, A. W., "Social Institutions and Nuclear Energy," Science,
vol. 177, pp. 27-34, July 7, 1972.

Weyl, P. K., "Temperature Distribution of Effluent," Technical Report
9, Marine Sciences Research Center, State University of New York,
Stony Brook, New York, August 1971.

Williams, G. C., Mitton, J. B., Suchanek, T. H., Gelelein, N., Gross-
man, C., Pearce, J., Young, J., Taylor, C. E., Mulstay, R., Hardy,
C. D., "Effects of a Steam-Electric Generating Plant on the Marine
Environment," Technical Report 10, Marine Sciences Research Center,
State University of New York, Stony Brook, New York, November 1971.

Zeller, E. J., Saunders, D. F., Angino, E. E., "Putting Radioactive Wastes on Ice," Science and Public Affairs, vol. 29, no. 1, January 1973.

1973 Suggested State Legislation, Vol. XXXII, Council of State Governments, Lexington, Kentucky, PP. 359-373.

CHAPTER 3

Urban Markets

It seems pertinent to begin to broaden somewhat the perspective of these working groups and begin to investigate other important facets of an urban technology which contribute heavily to the ultimate transfer of the technology. One such area is the actual dollar value of the marketplace for the times typically discussed in the panel sessions. This then will begin to answer some of the questions (though certainly not all) raised in the earlier chapters regarding funding needs, levels, expenditures. (Most of this portion of the current report is abstracted from Reference 1)

In the past the industrial and research communities have often asserted that the civil sector was not interested in innovative approaches and that, even if they were, the potential market for goods and services was too fragmented and too small for the requisite risk taking. Therefore, they have generally overlooked metropolitan markets and maintained an intensive sales effort to their single customer, the federal government, and then primarily within the defense-military complex; that is, Department of Defense, National Aeronautics and Space Administration and the Atomic Energy Commission where most of the money is spent (both in terms of total and R&D dollars).

This is not to say that new improved products were not developed or purchased by cities or that cities which were searching for products found none available. It is well recognized that the efforts of industrial and institutional research have been able to develop, for example, sophisticated control systems to automate transit systems, increasingly effective smokestack precipitators and new methods of

147

secondary material recovery from solid wastes. Additional evidence, of course, is available in the outputs of many of the working groups themselves. Our emphasis now is to see that additional possibilities exist and in that light explore an urban market which is considerably different from what might first be imagined.

In light of recent changes in national priorities, especially with regard to large-scale space, missile, and defense programs[*], it is pertinent to examine carefully these metropolitan markets to see what, in fact, is happening. To do so properly, we must define what might loosely be called a technology-intensive market. This can be generally thought of as composed of the products purchased in high-technology areas. For our purposes, the most important areas are sewage treatment, health care (which includes anti-pollution equipment and hospital care), transit, police, sanitation, and fire.[**] Our reasons for selecting these are twofold. Based on the dollar expenditures, they make up the largest part of the market as we will see. The local spending in these areas amounts to an urban technology program of considerable magnitude. Moreover, there exist federal counterparts in all these areas so that some match-up is offered in the development of the total picture for technology-intensive products. Generally, these opportunity areas have been those heavily supported by Federal-State grants which have guarantees and waiver-of-debt limit requirements that have allowed funds to be more readily available without heavy central control.

The other basic reason may be suggested by evaluation of local problems. Surely the goods and services represented by these generic topics are high on the priority list of most cities and have therefore been given most attention. Industry, then, does well, as we will see,

---

[*]In view of new and important energy research now being contemplated, some of these judgments might have to be tempered -- but, at most, qualitatively.

[**]We may note that this covers most, but not all, of the sessions treated in the workshops. The expenditures in the other areas do not contribute significantly to the overall picture.

in addressing needs associated with these topics. Definition of these items are cited in the Addendum to this chapter and come from cited References 2, 3, and 4.

In developing the data for our exploration (which comes largely from summaries of city budgets available in the aforementioned references, it is important to include two sets of expenditures. Generally speaking, we usually identify technology-intensive products in any city budget with the corresponding caputal budget items. These include construction projects (like sewage treatment plants) or equipment purchases having an expected life of five or more years. However, as part of current operations, considerable outlays occur for supplies, materials, and contracted services which likewise may be technically oriented. Thus, our data, so generated, include both capital and current expenditures which can be considered pertinent to our study.

Such data have been gathered for all cities for the last 10 years. The total technology-intensive market is shown in Figure 1. To lend perspective to the total and for comparison purposes so that a measure of its magnitude can be appreciated, the outlays for manned space flights -- the Apollo Program -- are also shown for the same time period. We see that the total urban market -- now approaching $5 billion annually, rivals the Apollo Program at its peak. As may be observed, with increasing emphasis on the cities and their future, it may be expected that this will be growing. It then becomes clear why the industrial community has come calling on the urban sector. We might point out that the totals reflect only city expenditures. Federal impacts and specialized national programs dealing with urban priorities are described later.

It is useful to break down this market into its important programmatic components according to those most important technology-intensive areas as cited above. We do so in Figure 2 for the fiscal year 1971 (the latest for which complete data are available). Sewage treatment , with its highest investment in capital expenditures -- new

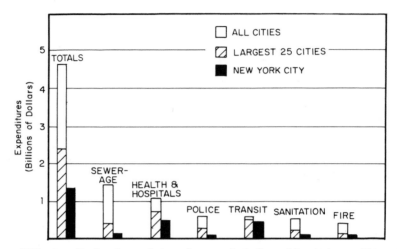

FIG. 1.   Technology-intensive market for all cities. (From Refs. 2,3,4.)

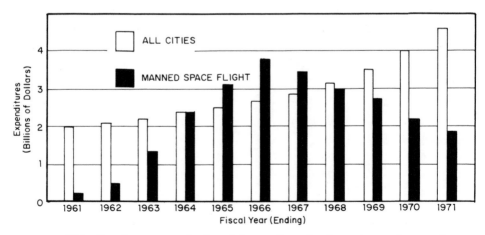

FIG. 2.   Programmatic breakdown of technology-intensive market for fiscal year ending 1971. (From Refs. 4,5.)

plants and products for water pollution abatement -- clearly dominates
the total picture.   This is not unexpected when we consider the magnitude of water treatment problems in local communities.   The health
and hospital area follows and is largely composed of new equipment for
both hospitals and air pollution abatement. With the modern available
technology such products are expensive and thus give rise to a large
market. The remaining areas are roughly equal in total expenditures.
Details of the market suggest new vehicles and control equipment (including computers) for the police, transit, and fire services. Sanitation, in addition to collection trucks and associated equipment also
includes new disposal plants (although on a much smaller scale than
that associated with sewage). In time, as advanced processes for recycling come on line, we may expect this last to grow considerably.

Due to the success of Public Technology, Inc., special new considerations are being given to our larger municipalities. First suggested in Reference 5, a big-city consortium of the 25 largest urban
markets is under development.   Its basic goals are similar to those
established by PTI and will be organized in conjunction with them.
Its particular purpose will be to address those issues especially
germane to our largest cities. As with PTI, projects and products
developed will be user oriented to assure acceptance.   Through a defined aggressive market aggregation resulting from the formalization
of a consortium, these major cities will interact with industry, the
universities, and the federal government to define problems, give direction to new and ongoing research, and most importantly, monitor developments and installations to effect full-scale technology transfer.

Thus it is of interest to look at some sub-markets. In Figure 2,
we also display the expenditures for these 25 largest urban markets.
In Table 1, a breakdown of these cities is shown, along with their
population. We can say, then, that these cities, having approximately
15% of the total United States population and 21% of the urban population, spend approximately 50% of the urban dollars. From the industrial point of view, these figures begin to address the problem of a
disaggregated market. Rather than selling to some 18,000 cities, cor-

TABLE 1

The Technology-Intensive Market[a] in the
25 Largest U.S. Cities

City	1970 Population (1000's)	Total technology-intensive expenditures in 1971 (millions of dollars)
New York	7896	1304
Chicago	3369	108
Los Angeles	2810	71
Philadelphia	1950	86
Detroit	1514	109
Houston	1233	30
Baltimore	906	55
Dallas	844	28
Washington, D.C.	756	111
Cleveland	751	52
Indianapolis	745	18
Milwaukee	717	27
San Francisco	716	76
San Diego	697	25
San Antonio	654	13
Boston	641	48
Honolulu	631	26
Memphis	624	39
St. Louis	622	28
New Orleans	593	23
Phoenix	582	11
Columbus	540	16
Seattle	531	38
Pittsburgh	520	12
Denver	515	24
Total	31,356	2,376
Total U.S.:	203,212	4,754

[a]Technology-intensive market is defined as the goods, products, and equipment for sewage, health, hospitals, police, transit, sanitation, and fire.

porations can begin to focus on a rather discrete number and still avail themselves of a considerable market total. Smaller cities also have needs for some of these advanced products; mechanisms such as PTI must be under continual development so that their progress at least roughly matches that of the large municipalities.

Finally, it is pertinent here to depict the New York City market. With 5% of the urban population, it spends 25% of the urban dollars as may be seen in **Figure** 2. It is no wonder that New York, by itself, can be a formidable aggregated market for the urban sector and is so viewed by the corporate institutions.

Although emphasis here is on the city market, federal components cannot be overlooked. Historically, the federal government has been expending dollars over the years for innovative projects and has been willing to experiment with new applications in new areas of endeavor. It has been willing, where both industry and local government have not, to take risks and fund research for products and systems that have only limited probability of success. This notion of risk is an important inhibitor to technology transfer and yet has simultaneously given rise to new institutions for urban research. In any case, industry in looking for front-end funds to enter this new urban market has attempted to return to their single federal customer with its new ideas.

The other important reason stems from this question of risks and concerns the federal dollar component to the technology-intensive areas cited above. A brief review of this piece of the market in fiscal year 1971 suggests that obligations for research and development by the departments of Commerce, Defense (Corps of Engineers of the United States Army), Health, Education, and Welfare, Housing and Urban Development, Interior, Justice, and Transportation, and agencies such as the Environmental Protection Agency, Atomic Energy Commission, National Science Foundation, have totalled at least $500 million for the urban market. The largest expenditures have been in those areas paralleling the city market: pollution abatement, health, etc.

In addition, we must consider the programs of general and specific revenue sharing. When viewed as new federal inputs to city budgets, such elements make it all the more attractive to industry. To round out this discussion we treat them here briefly.

Under specific revenue sharing, it is suggested that roughly $5 billion would be made available to cities for the technology areas cited above. Most important in this regard is the elimination of the usual federal matching requirements. No matter how allocated, many cities will receive considerable funds through general revenue sharing. While certainly not all can (or even should) go to technology-intensive items, if ratios of such expenditures to total expenditures remain roughly constant, it can be expected that of the $30 billion authorized for the five-year program in fiscal years, 1973-1977, approximately $3 billion will be added to this high-technology market. Again, this further reinforces the notion of a growing and strong marketplace for industry.

REFERENCES

1. Fox, H., "Technology and the City: Opportunities and Problems," City Almanac, New School for Social Research, New York, October 1974.

2. U.S. Bureau of the Census, "Statistical Abstract of the United States, Washington, D.C., Annual.

3. U.S. Bureau of the Census, "Governmental Finance," Washington, D.C., Annual.

4. U.S. Bureau of the Census, "City Government Finance," Washington, D.C., Annual.

5. Rees, C. and Fox, H., "Can Urban Areas Survive in a Population and Resource Limited World?", paper presented at 1971 Annual Meeting of the American Association for the Advancement of Science, Philadelphia, Pennsylvania.

ADDENDUM

BASIC DEFINITIONS (ADAPTED FROM REFERENCES 2, 3 AND 4)

Capitol Outlay - Direct expenditure for contract or force account contribution of buildings, roads, and other improvements, and for pur-

chase of equipment, land, and existing structures. Includes amounts
for addition, replacements, and major alterations to fixed works and
structures. However, expenditures for repairs to such works and structures are classified as current operating expenditures.

Construction - Production of fixed works, structures, additions, replacements, and major alterations thereto, including planning and design of specific projects, site improvements, and provision of equipment, and facilities that are integral parts of a structure. Includes
both contract and force account construction.

Current Operations - Direct expenditure for -ompensation of officers
and employees and for supplies, materials, and contractural services,
except amounts for capital outlay.

Equipment - Apparatus, furnishings, motor vehicles, office machines
and the like, having an expected life of more than five years. Equipment expenditure consists only of amounts for purchase of equipment.
Rental and repair expenditures are classified as current operation
expenditures.

Fire Protection - City fire fighting organization and auxiliary services, inspection for fire hazards and other fire prevention activities. Includes cost of fire fighting facilities such as fire hydrants
and water.

Health - Health services other than hospital care including health
research, clinics, nurseries, immunization and other categorical, environmental, and general public health activities.

Hospitals - Establishment and operation of hospital facilities, provision of hospital care, and support of other public or private hospitals.

Personnel Services - Amounts paid for compensation of city officers
and employees.

Police Protection - Preservation of law and order and traffic safety.
Includes police patrols and communication, crime prevention activities, detention and custody of persons awaiting trial, vehicle inspection, etc.

Sanitation (other than sewage) - Street cleaning and collection and
disposal of garbage and other waste. Sanitary engineering, smoke regulation and other health activities are classified under Health.

Sewerage - Sanitary and storm sewers, sewage disposal facilities, and
services and payments to other local governments for such purposes.

Transit Utility Expenditure - Expenditures for construction or acquisition of utility facilities or equipment, for production and distribution of utility commodities and services, and for interest on debt.

A. INTRODUCTION

Like the summary of the results of the working groups at UTC 2, this final chapter focuses on several elements. The first is a continuation of the notion of dominant inhibitors which was first introduced in Reference 1. This will be followed by an overall program review and will include the results of a questionnaire used at the conference. Finally, some suggestions are offered for improving the mechanism initiated at UTC 2, continued at UTC 3 and projected for future conferences.

B. INHIBITORS

Let us re-introduce here the inhibitor categories first defined in Reference 1. One basic type is that of development in its broadest sense. This concerns the continued engineering of products or systems which are not ready for full-scale implementation but for which a need has been identified. The market mechanism -- through government spending (as cited in Chapter 3) and/or private industry investment -- have not taken hold to establish a firm basis for extensive product or software manufacture. Another inhibitor is that of external policy constraints. As suggested in Reference 1, these are largely political problems and relate closely to the external policy issues cited in Figure 1 of the Introduction. Also, we may identify internal local government education as a basic inhibitor to the transfer process. While this is a thread common to almost all sessions, this arose as the dominant problem area in some working groups. We should be

157

careful to note there that the education called for must be directed
to both the industrial and the urban community, the former, to fully
understand the needs, the latter to understand the technology available for implementation.

The panels and their relation to these inhibitors is shown in
Figure 1. The rationale for such placement is presented below in our
summary of the working groups.

Let us first consider the developmental area. Educational technology, for all its great press, has yet to show positive results.
New cost-effective developments must be made to realize its promise.
Traditional teacher-lecture-recitation systems still appear less expensive. With the dramatic drop in the birth rate and the continual
closing of public and private schools, from elementary level through
college, the educational establishment must look to these techniques

DOMINANT INHIBITORS

DEVELOPMENT

EDUCATION
ERTS
FIRE COMMUNICATION
POLICE VEHICLES

EXTERNAL POLICY

CABLE TV
POWERPLANT SITING

INTERNAL EDUCATION

AIRPORT SECURITY
BUS TRANSPORT
EMERGENCY MEDICAL CARE
SOLID WASTE

FIG 1. Dominant Inhibitors.

(and others) for its very survival. We may see a new breed of educator in the coming years, not so much lecturer as software developer. This becomes viable only when the experiments cited in the problem session show their real utility.

Even with the large market for police vehicles cited at UTC 2 and mentioned here in both the problem session and the expenditure summaries in Chapter 3, manufacturers and local police forces are still turning to standard sedans. We might note that in tracking this problem to its second appearance at UTC 3, no new information has been exchanged and that many of the same issues have been aired. It is still not clear what is needed; surely, new developments in standards and purchasing through aggregation can at least begin to solve many of the problems noted in Chapter 1.

Fireground communications equipment has always been cited as a technology which could be addressed if, for example, standardization in specifications was available. This panel session, as well as long-term studies by Public Technology, Inc., have begun to address this rather well defined problem. Constant exposure through mechanisms such as this conference will, hopefully, set the stage for industrial development of the required products.

As noted earlier, the purpose of introducing the session on Earth Resource Technology Satellites (ERTS) was to expose a new technology to local government. The ultimate utility of ERTS remains to be seen. City managers can have important inputs to these powerful systems only through greater understanding; future developments can be geared to their needs as remote sensing becomes established as a viable tool for pollution abatement.

The two panel sessions dominated by external policy inhibitors -- cable television and power plant siting -- have not changed categories from UTC 2 to UTC 3. For cable systems, franchising difficulties, and the attendant political problems remain at the fore. Interaction of local government with the citizenry and the implementation of cable are still critical issues. One other area was discussed during the panel which is worthy of repetition here -- economic viability is not as easy to prove as might have been expected, especially if we look at the multitude of desired services (see Reference 1).

With the energy crisis likely to remain a problem in the coming decade, the resolution of the political problems of power plant sit-int becomes even more critical. The tradeoffs between ecology and power needs have to be carefully explained to communities. It must be pointed out, unequivocally, that the public cannot always have it both ways -- power plants which do not in any way impinge on their environment and yet satisfy their increasing demand for energy. Continued government streamlining of the licensing procedures may improve the situation and go a long way toward its ultimate resolution.

Finally, let us review the sessions in the education-inhibitor category. New processes were identified in the solid waste session. These included new collection devices (hard technology) and new management schemes for improving this labor-intensive service (soft technology). Highlighting these elements during the working session begins to suggest to many municipalities that study must be undertaken to implement them. In terms of the year-by-year tracking of this area, we might note that substantive accomplishments were cited which can be used effectively in almost all areas of the country. Furthermore, the management scheme discussed -- management-by-objectives -- is exactly the one put forth at UTC 2. In a sense then, we did well to eliminate a general management working group; these applications to real situations are obviously more useful than theoretical discussions.[*]

According to current standards, much of the technology required for effective airport security already exists. An important function of a working group in an area such as this would be dissemination; much of the discussion tended to accomplish this and the session appeared to be useful for the attendees.

---

[*]Direct management applications to a variety of situations were presented during the plenary session at the conference. These results are available in Reference 2.

Medical care delivery, one component of which was addressed at UTC 2, again fell into the education category. Viable systems are being implemented throughout the country as this problem begins to reach public attention. The technology exists, jurisdictional problems are obvious, but careful planning can overcome many of these difficulties.

The working group on bus transportation, like the ERTS session, was mainly expository. The techniques cited were presented with a wealth of examples and offered important data germane to the problems of cost, population, vehicles, etc. Our purpose here was to offer the city manager as wide a variety of options as possible to provide effective bus transportation for his locality. It is clear that substantial education of local city management is necessary to intelligently select and implement the choices. Furthermore, additional studies were presented during the plenary session (2) and, together with this working group, offers the city planner a complete reference for transit selection and implementation.

This year's analysis, when coupled to the issue-oriented categories suggested in Chapter 1 and correlated with the results of UTC 2, leads to some important conclusions. The dominating themes for most of the sessions -- developmental issues paired with developmental inhibitors, and application issues paired with internal education -- are, in a sense, what may have been expected a priori. For the first set, high technology industry is still addressing the basic problems; it is still groping for standards, specifications and markets for the identified systems. In many cases, a language barrier exists between the urban manager and his technological counterpart which prevents effective translation of needs into products. When technology exists and can, in fact, solve real problems, local government must translate them for their application. Substantial understanding of the products possibly observing implementation in other localities, and molding the results to particular needs are all required and form a substantial education problem for city management.

C. PROGRAM REVIEW AND THE FUTURE

Many of the general problems of the workshop mechanism identified in Reference 1 were addressed here. These included a better match of panelists to the focused study of a single problem, elimination of the problem-statement-consensus approach, and the limitation on panel size.

Overall, it can be said that these difficulties were avoided in this second attempt at effective working groups. As might be expected in an iterative process such as this, new problems arose which should be treated in the future. The most disconcerting of these was the unevenness of the problem statements and panel summaries. A more viable technique for generating the written material might be a combination of the formats of both UTC 2 and UTC 3. Thus we suggest a single author for all materials, who would work closely with the selected chairmen to draw on their expertise. This would assure completeness of the problem statements. The single author, presumably a trained documenter, would also be responsible for the panel summaries. Thus, material could be culled from the working groups which might be used toward the ultimate goal of the working group process -- technology transfer.

Aside from the comments above, it must be said that the panels in general were remarkably successful. Whether of the working group type or the tutorial cast, they performed their missions well. To assess, at least in a preliminary way, the effectiveness of the panels, questionnaires were distributed to all participants (see Exhibit 1). The sampling, unfortunately, was quite small; apparently the chairmen did not stress the importance of this survey on the audience (which numbered roughly 40 or more per session). The results, panel-by-panel, with appropriate totals, are displayed in Table 1. Because of the small sampling per session, let us focus on the totals for several of the categories in the questionnaire. First, in terms of respondents, just under half were from the government sector, with the remainder from high-technology industry and universities; thus we can feel sure that the results obtained are representative of the several communities in attendance.

The general concept of the working groups appears highly effective. Questions 5, 6 and 7 address this issue, and it would seem that the results suggest that there is overwhelming favor with the mechanism. Notwithstanding some of the comments made earlier, most of the respondents (70%) agreed that the particular problem statement chosen for discussion was satisfactory and addressed their needs (question 9). Furthermore, panel selection likewise seemed more than adequate; responses to question 11 indicate 80% felt that the panel was effective. This should give us confidence to continue the method of selection for both the problem statements and participants in the coming years. The notion of audience reaction and discussion has still not settled well with the meeting attendees. It appears that they are not quite ready to work and join in on a shirt-sleeve session, as evidenced by the answers to question 12.

The answers to questions 10 and 14 tell the real story of effectiveness. If no new information were to be disseminated and if no follow-up activities could be contemplated, our purpose would have been defeated. For these workshops to have had meaning so we could press for their continuation, the responses indicated in Table 2 were necessary. The fact that most respondents garnered new facts and want to implement their findings within their own job contexts is most encouraging.

At this juncture, we feel that it may be useful to develop approaches for follow-up actions as was suggested by many respondents. We could then determine the long-range effectiveness of this type of activity and establish either a mechanism for additional in-depth studies if warranted or recommend the closure of a particular subject.

REFERENCES

1. Fox, H., "Urban Technology: A Primer on Problems, Vol. 1", Marcel Dekker, Inc., New York, 1973.

2. "A Collection of Technical Papers," Third Urban Technology Conference and Technical Display, Boston, Mass., September 1973; American Institute of Aeronautics and Astronautics, New York, 1973.

EXHIBIT 1

WORKING GROUP QUESTIONNAIRE

As part of the study for the National Science Foundation Grant supporting the various working groups,
we are investigating the efficacy of this mechanism
for Technology Transfer. We would appreciate your
cooperation and response to these questions. PLEASE
COMPLETE AND RETURN TO THE REPORTER(OR PLACE IN THE
BOX PROVIDED)BEFORE YOU LEAVE TODAY. Thank you!

1. Title of the Working Group _____

2. Personal identification (withhold if necessary; otherwise, please
    include for followup purposes)

3. (a) Name _____

    (b) Organization _____

3. I am in
    (a) Industry ____
    (b) University ____
    (c) Non-profit Research Corporation or Foundation ____
    (d) Federal Government ____
    (e) State Government ____
    (f) City Government ____
    (g) County Government ____
    (h) Other (please specify) _____

4. My job primarily involves
    (a) Research ____
    (b) Development ____
    (c) Management ____
    (d) Contracting ____
    (e) Purchasing ____
    (f) Other (please specify) _____

5. In general, the concept of the Working Groups is:

    (a) a good one, and assists both industry and government. _____
    (b) a faire one. _____
    (c) a poor one which should probably be reworked substantially
        or eliminated. ____

6. In general, the use of single-topic problem statements is:

    (a) a good one which permits useful, in-depth discussion. ____
    (b) a fair one. _____
    (c) a poor one which should be eliminated and multiple issues
        in a discipline be discussed. _____

7. In general, is the combination of single-topic Problem State-
    ments and Working Group panel format useful?

    (a) Yes ____
    (b) No ____
    (c) If not, how should the Groups be organized? _____

    _____

    _____

8. I read the Problem Statement.

    (a) Yes ____
    (b) No ____

9. The particular Problem Statement is:

    (a) Too broad ____
    (b) Too specific ____
    (c) Too technical ____
    (d) Not technical enough ____
    (e) Satisfactory ____

    I have the following suggestions for improvement: _____

    _____

    _____

10. I learned

    (a) Something new ____
    (b) Nothing new ____

11. The panelists were

    (a) effective ____
    (b) fair ____
    (c) ineffective ____
    (d) I have the following suggestions for improvement _____

    _____

    _____

12. The audience participation was

    (a) effective ____
    (b) fair ____
    (c) ineffective ____

13. My job function includes problems paralleling this working group.

    (a) Yes ____
    (b) No ____

14. I plan follow-on action in my job

     (a) Yes _____
     (b) No _____
     (c) Action to be taken _____

     _____

     _____

15. (d) My best guess at the effectiveness of my action _____

     _____

     _____

15. In addition to the above, I have the following specific sug-
     gestions on the working group method (e.g., subject matter,
     arrangements, procedures, etc.):

     _____

     _____

     _____

     _____

(Please use other side for further comments.)

TABLE 1

Results of Questionnaire at UTC 3 Working Groups*

Question	Airport security (1)	Bus transit (12)	Cable TV (14)	Edu. tech. (8)	ERTS (10)	Fire-ground comm. (8)	Emergency med. care (6)	Police vehicles (14)	Power plant siting (14)	Solid waste (22)	Totals (103)
3. (a)				3	4	2	2	2	2	4	19
(b)		3	2	4				1	1	1	12
(c)	1	2	3	1	2			3	3	2	16
(d)		1	1		2	1		1	1	1	8
(e)		1					1	1	1	1	5
(f)		3	4		1	3	1	5		10	27
(g)		2					1				3
(h)		1	3		2	1	2	1	1	4	15
4. (a)		5	5	2	2	1		1	6	6	28
(b)		3	3	2	3	2	1	3		3	20
(c)		6	6	2	1	2	4	7	4	10	42
(d)		1						1			2
(e)					1			2			3
(f)	1			3	4	4	2	1		4	19
5. (a)	1	10	12	8	8	7	4	11	6	22	89
(b)			1		1	1	1	1	2		7
(c)							1				1
6. (a)	1	6	12	8	8	8	5	11	7	22	88
(b)		3	1		1			1	1		7
(c)		1									1
7. (a)	1	8	11	8	7	8	6	12	8	22	91
(b)		1	1								2
8. (a)	1	6	8	7	9	8	4	12	7	18	80
(b)		1	5	1	1		2			3	13

TABLE 1 (CONT.)

Question	Airport security (1)	Bus transit (12)	Cable TV (14)	Edu. tech. (8)	ERTS (10)	Fire-ground comm. (8)	Emergency med. care (6)	Police vehicles (14)	Power plant siting (14)	Solid waste (22)	Totals (103)
9. (a)		2	1	1	1		1	3	3	1	13
(b)						1				1	2
(c)											0
(d)	1	1	6	1		1	3	1	2	3	9
(e)		7		5	8	7		7	3	12	59
10. (a)	1	10	12	7	10	8	4	11	6	20	89
(b)			1	1			1	1	2		6
11. (a)	1	5	12	7	5	8	5	10	6	20	79
(b)		6	1	1	5			4	2		19
(c)											0
12. (a)		4	9	2	2	5	2	3	6	17	50
(b)	1	5	4	6	6	2	2	9	1	3	39
(c)		2			1		1	2	1	1	8
13. (a)	1	7	10	5	8	6	5	10	8	12	71
(b)		2	3	2	2	1	1	2		6	20
14. (a)	1	5	8	4	5	5	3	3	7	16	57
(b)		3	2	2	3		1	3		3	17

*Numbers in parantheses beneath panel titles indicate number of respondents.

WORKING GROUP PANELISTS

AIRPORT SECURITY

Chairman: J. Donald Reilly, Executive Vice President
            Airport Operators Council International, Inc.
            Washington, D.C.

Panelists: Richard Mettler, Manager
            Los Angeles International Airport

            Harry Murphy, Director, Office of Security
            Air Transport Association

            James Murphy, Director, Office of Air Trans-
              portation Security
            Federal Aviation Administration

            John Taylor, City Manager
            Kansas City, Missouri

AIR/WATER POLLUTION ABATEMENT UTILIZING
EARTH OBSERVATION SATELLITES

Chairman: Dr. Lawrence R. Greenwood
            NASA Langley Research Center
            Hampton, Virginia

Panelists: Joseph M. Carlson, Asst. to the Sr. Vice President
            Public Technology, Inc.

            Donald C. Holmes, Assoc. Deputy Asst. Administrator
            Environmental Protection Agency
            Washington, D.C.

            Dennis R. Bates, Director, Dept. of Health and
              and Environmental Protection
            Council of Governments

            Ray Goode, County Manager
            Dade County, Florida

169

BUS TRANSPORTATION SYSTEMS

Chairman: Fred B. Burke
            Public Technology, Inc.

Panelists: Ronald Fisher
            Urban Mass Transportation Administration

            Stanley Rosen
            Chase, Rosen & Wallace, Inc.

            Costis Toregas
            Public Technology, Inc.

            E. Robert Turner, City Manager
            Cincinnati, Ohio

CABLE TELEVISION

Chairman: Joseph F. Coates
            Office of Technology Assessment
            United States Congress

Panelists: Walter S. Baer
            Rand Corporation

            Michael Botein, Cable TV Bureau
            Federal Communications Commission

            Edward Deagle
            Cable TV Information Center
            New York, New York

            James A. Lippke, Editor, "Cable Management
              Engineering"
            Broad Band Information Services
            New York, New York

            Frank Young, CATV Project Director
            National League of Cities

EDUCATIONAL TECHNOLOGY

Chairman: James D. Koerner
            Alfred P. Sloan Foundation
            New York, New York

Panelists: Dr. Robert Filep, Director, National Center
              for Educational Technology
            U.S. Office of Education
            Washington, D.C.

Dr. Norman Dahl (retired)
Ford Foundation

Joseph Orndorff, Director
Community Services
Dayton, Ohio

Dr. Theodore K. Steele, Vice President of
  Academic Affairs
New York Institute of Technology
Old Westbury, New York

FIREGROUND COMMUNICATIONS

Chairman: Raymond C. Picard, Chief
            Huntington Beach Fire Department
            Huntington Beach, California

Panelists: Martin Grimes, Director, Fire Service Division
            National Fire Protection Association
            Boston, Massachusetts

            Alred J. Mellow, Director of Communications
            Providence, Rhode Island

            George H. Paul, Chief
            Boston Fire Department
            Boston, Massachusetts

            Roger Rowe, Project Director
            Public Technology, Inc.

MEDICAL CARE DELIVERY SYSTEMS

Chairman: John G. Veneman
            Bank of America Associates Center
            San Francisco, California

Panelists: Peter J. Christiano, City Administrator
            Southfield, Michigan

            Frederick J. Lewis, Jr.
            Highway Safety Management Specialist
            National Highway Traffic Safety Administration

            Robert Patricelli, Vice President
            Hartford Process, Inc.

            George Podgorny, M.D., Director of Emergency Services
            Forsythe Memorial Hospital
            Winston-Salem, North Carolina

POLICE VEHICLE TECHNOLOGY

Chairman: David R. Powell
            Law Enforcement Assistance Administration
            United States Department of Justice
            New York, New York

Panelists: Gino D'Angelo, Director of Fiscal Management
            New York State Police

            Peter Korn, City Business Manager
            Jersey City, New Jersey

            A. F. Munroe, National Account Executive
            Lincoln-Mercury Division of Ford Motors

            G. R. Wynne, Director, Police Transportation
            Los Angeles, California

            Francis Zunno, Asst. Director, Research Division
            IACP

POWER PLANT SITING

Chairman: Dr. Seville Chapman, Director, Assembly
                Scientific Staff
            New York State Legislature
            Albany, New York

Panelists: David J. Rose, Professor
            Massachusetts Institute of Technology

            Harry G. Woodbury, Executive Vice President
            Consolidated Edison Company
            New York, New York

            Harry Dyer, Assistant to the County Manager
            Dade County, Florida

            Robert F. Carroll, City Desk
            New York Daily News
            New York, New York

SOLID WASTE COLLECTION TECHNOLOGY

Chairman: David H. Marks, Director
            Civil Engineering Systems Laboratory
            Massachusetts Institute of Technology

Panelists: Jon Liebman, Professor
            Department of Civil Engineering
            University of Illinois at Urbana

James Moar, Director, Bureau of Industrial
   Engineers
Environmental Protection Agency
New York, New York

Marc Straiger, Director, Dept. of Public Works
Scottsdale, Arizona

David Wilson, Professor
Department of Mechanical Engineering
Massachusetts Institute of Technology

John Starr, Vice President, Research and Development
SEA Industries
Boston, Massachusetts

James Buell
Public Technology, Inc.